RAW FOODS

**Simple and
Machine Free Recipes
for Every Day**

FOR BUSY PEOPLE

by Jordan Maerin

5th Anniversary Edition

Published by
Pure Energy Publishing
Sacramento, CA

This book is dedicated to
The three people who got me started:

Raymond Francis, MSc, RNC
Nancy Gordon, LCSW
Aaron Howard

Cover Design: Vanesa Duran Christman
Illustrations: Bernadine Saint-Auguste

ISBN-13: 978-0-9774858-6-4
Third Edition, 5th Anniversary, 2009

Acknowledgements:
Thanks to everyone who encouraged and inspired me and gave me good
ideas and feedback, including: Rob Titus, Aaron Howard,
Raymond Francis, Brian Anderson, Kimberly Dark, Nancy Gordon,
Chris O'Loughlin, the entire staff of Nature's First Law, and all those
who participated in the book's pre-sale. And most of all to my wife,
LaDawn, for her unwavering support and faith.

Disclaimer:
The responsibility for any adverse detoxification effects or
consequences resulting from the use of any suggestions described
hereafter lies not with the author or distributors of this book. This book
is not intended as medical advice. By following any suggested dietary
program, you are prescribing for yourself, which is your right.

TABLE OF CONTENTS

Raw Foods for Busy People

FOREWORD
To the 5th Anniversary edition

When *Raw Foods for Busy People* was first released, in the summer of 2004, it was a departure from the raw food recipe books that had been available before. It was a simple book, but not so simple as to be boring or monotonous. There were certainly other simple recipe books on the market, but none that were titled and marketed as such. It was time for this sort of book, and the following year, I became aware of two other books with the same theme, including Brian Au's *Raw in Ten Minutes* and Jennifer Cornbleet's *Raw Foods Made Easy for 1 or 2 People*. The time had arrived to combine *simple* and *interesting* in the world of raw foods, and there was a new kind of market waiting to receive it.

The raw food diet originally became popular in the U.S., through the work of Ann Wigmore, Viktor Kulvinskas and Raychel Solomon, because of its potential to help people dramatically heal from serious diseases like cancer, diabetes, and MS, to name just a few, and more recently chronic fatigue, fibromyalgia and acid reflux. Therefore, all the recipe books were created to appeal to this market, in two ways. First, for the strict health regimen itself, which made the recipes less than palatable and often monotonous (e.g. just eat homegrown sprouts and sprinkle everything with liquid aminos). And second, with the assumption that the followers of the diet would be doing it *for life* and therefore would want the most elaborate gourmet recipes possible, including those that mimicked popular cooked foods (e.g. Portobello meatloaf, pot pies, chocolate cakes). In both cases, this amounted to a labor-intensive lifestyle and some intimidating recipe books and classes.

Enter the new age of raw foods, when people who are not terribly ill are using raw foods to achieve optimal health – people like David Wolfe of Sunfood Nutrition and Thor Bazler of Raw Power (both co-founders of Nature's First Law), as well as more recent authors of raw food recipe books, including myself. The fact that the raw food diet has been embraced by people who are already relatively healthy has changed everything, including how recipe books are written and marketed. There is now even an exclusive, celebrity-type status enjoyed by certain raw food chefs and authors, such as Juliano, author of *RAW: The Uncook Book* and purveyor of Planet Raw restaurant in Santa Monica, and Matthew Kenney and Sarma Melngailis of Pure Food and Wine in Manhattan, authors of *Raw Food Real World*.

The time has arrived to celebrate the diverse coalition of people who are embracing different types of raw food diets for many different reasons: for healing, weight loss, spiritual growth, age reversal, overall rejuvenation and just plain fun.

I originally wrote *Raw Foods for Busy People* for my home-delivery customers in San Diego, only two of whom were seriously ill, and all of whom were busy people. I am happy to have made my contribution, and equally happy to have seen the awareness of raw foods grow so much in this country in the past several years. I look forward to the day when raw foods are taken for granted as a *necessary* part of everyone's pursuit of optimal health, because that's exactly what they are.

Jordan Maerin
Sacramento, California
March 24, 2009

Raw food is glamorous: the 2005 cover of *Raw Food Real World*.

PREFACE

Like a growing number of enthusiastically healthy people all over the world, switching to a raw food diet has given me a new lease on life!

At the age of 36 I was already experiencing signs of "aging", like widespread joint and back pain, chronic gum infections, constant indigestion and lack of energy. I felt like a wind-up toy that was winding inexorably *down.* I expected that I was just getting older and that my ailments would slowly worsen as I aged.

Culturally speaking, we often take this kind of physical deterioration for granted. How often have we shared "over the hill" jokes with our friends and family members?

Then I discovered the book *Never Be Sick Again* by Raymond Francis, M.Sc., R.N.C., and I suddenly had a glimpse into different possibilities. I came to see that the aches and pains I had been experiencing are not natural after all, though they are definitely, and tragically, the norm.

I subsequently discovered the writings of Dr. Norman Walker and Nature's First Law, and I was on my way to Paradise Health.

The high quantity of raw foods I've been eating is, in effect, new information for my body, which is speaking to me more loudly now that it knows I'm listening. In fact, I have come to prefer and *love* raw foods! Consequently, I've been learning about the processes of detoxification, and I am ever so grateful to people who make colon hygiene their priority and life's work. Thank you!

I have the energy of an adolescent again, and am enjoying a spiritual and emotional renaissance. I have expanded my expectations for my life, and for every single day I live. No more joint pains, gum infections, or indigestion. No more sinus headaches either, and sunburns are a thing of the past. Not only do I no longer feel sluggish, but exercising has become effortless, and I need much less sleep now than I used to. Cleansing my colon has relieved a lifetime of excruciating menstrual cramps for me, as well as the lower back aches I have suffered with for over a decade.

I had always been an enthusiastic vegetarian cook, both professionally and at home, so when I discovered raw foods I was excited to prepare and deliver them to my friends who were requesting them from me. I developed my raw repertoire by translating the recipes I had been using for years into raw versions, and then I studied gourmet raw recipe books and learned some new tricks. En route, I made great friends with my brand new machines: my food processor, dehydrator, juicer and Saladacco spiralizer.

After almost a year of preparing gourmet raw foods and working at my delivery business fulltime, however, I realized that I missed the simplicity of raw foods. Furthermore, I realized that most people wouldn't be able to spend the kind of time and energy I had been spending preparing raw gourmet foods every day of the week. Realizing that, I immediately made it my priority to develop a more simple and efficient daily routine for preparing tasty raw foods. My own return to a more simple raw diet has been very enjoyable for me, and it is my intention to help others create a simple raw food repertoire that they can maintain for the long run.

This book represents a compromise between simplicity and variety, ease and creativity. May it help you and your family on your path to Paradise Health!

INTRODUCTION

Let's face it. Busy people do not like to prepare food. We generally eat out. A lot.

If you want to eat raw foods but do not want to prepare anything yourself, then you'll subsist on fresh raw fruit and frequent your local salad bars. And if you're lucky, you'll live near a raw food restaurant. End of story.

However, there are many easy ways to enjoy more variety while eating raw foods. In this book, I discuss strategies for eating out; direct you to some mail order resources for raw prepared foods; and, yes, encourage you to learn some very simple dishes that you can prepare for yourself.

Even the busiest people enjoy some variety in the foods they eat, especially over the long run. Helping you achieve Paradise Health, happily and conveniently, is what this book is all about.

I had two reasons for writing this book.

First, I want to remove the last vestige of an excuse for you to resist embracing the raw food diet: the prep time factor.

Secondly, I want to inspire you to become as comfortably functional preparing raw foods in your kitchen as you ever have been preparing cooked foods (maybe even more so!).

Let me give you an example of what I mean. Imagine wanting to prepare a grilled cheese sandwich. Do you refer to a cookbook to find out how much butter you should use on the bread? Do you get out your scale and ask your guest exactly how many ounces of cheese they want on their sandwich? Do you rely on a thermometer to tell you when your skillet is ready to receive the sandwich? Do you again consult a cookbook to find out exactly how long the sandwich should remain on the hot skillet before flipping it to the other side? Of course not!

Instead, you easily assemble the ingredients, eyeball the amount of butter and cheese, throw the sandwich onto the skillet when you're ready, and then peek underneath the bottom piece of bread to determine when you want to flip it.

These have become easy, comfortable rituals, whatever we've learned to do in our kitchens over the course of our lifetimes. It's an ease that we take for granted, until the day we discover a whole new way of eating, like the raw food diet. A new direction like this seems like a curve ball, a speed bump. Suddenly, we feel that the rules have changed, the restrictions multiplied, the machinery become unfamiliar.

With the help of this book, you'll discover that raw food preparation takes much less time than you'd thought. And I've put in some of the time and energy for you, by translating, compiling and creating some very simple recipes, and consolidating them into types that will be easy for you to remember and duplicate.

With this book as your guide, you'll never again come home after an exhausting day and think, "I don't have the time and energy to make something healthy to eat."

Think of this book as your launching pad, as you discover the ease and comfort of preparing the most nutritious foods that nature has to offer, within the comfort of your own home.

Easy, natural, simple. This is the road to Paradise Health.

CHAPTER 1:
THE A.B.C.'S OF RAW

If you've picked up this book out of curiosity, you've probably already heard something about the healing and energizing powers of raw foods.

Raymond Francis, M.Sc., R.N.C., in his book, *Never Be Sick Again: Health is a Choice Learn How to Choose It*, explains why raw foods heal. Human disease manifests in many forms, but it has only one underlying cause: cellular malfunction. Cellular malfunction, in turn, has only two causes: deficiency and toxicity. Since cooking your food destroys vital nutrients and enzymes, the only way to give your cells all the nutrients they need and protect them from substances that are toxic or unusable, is to eat a diet that is at least 80% raw, and 100% whole and organic.

The evidence Raymond Francis presents includes his own recovery from near-fatal liver failure and chemical hepatitis, as well as an inspiring look at the healthiest peoples on the planet, including the disease-free Hunza people of the Himalayas.

Many Natural Hygienists and colon therapists agree with Raymond. The naturally high fiber content of raw foods is the key to a healthy digestive system and colon, and therefore to the absorption of optimum nutrition for every cell in your body. For more information, read *The Natural Hygiene Handbook* by the American Natural Hygiene Society, and *Colon Health: Key to a Vibrant Life* by Dr. Norman Walker.

DEFINITIONS OF "RAW"

Uncooked food – This is the literal definition: food that is unprocessed and unheated in any way. Not every product labeled "raw", however, is actually uncooked, because there are no food-industry-wide standards. You may see an energy bar or other product that is labeled "raw" because the combined product is uncooked, even though the various ingredients themselves may be cooked. Also, any nut that is machine-shelled, like cashews, may be cooked during the shelling process. Commercial dried fruit is also cooked at high temperatures for faster drying. Any product you buy in a jar that opens with a "pop" has been heat-sealed.

"Living" food – Live enzymes are the key to this definition of raw. Therefore, foods that have been cultured for high enzyme content are included here, even if the base of the food is cooked, as in the case of miso or Nama Shoyu soy sauce. By this definition, raw foods rich in enzyme-inhibitors, like nuts, seeds and legumes (lentils, etc.) will not be considered "living." To release the enzymes, nuts and sunflower seeds must be soaked in water for about 12 hours, and buckwheat (which is a gluten-free seed) and legumes must be sprouted, which can take a few days. Raw frozen foods maintain about 90% of their enzyme activity.

Leukocytosis-free food – This definition uses your body's reaction to foods as the standard for raw. When you eat cooked food on an empty stomach, your body's immune system will react and try to protect you from it, so any food that does not cause this reaction (leukocytosis) is raw and unharmful as far as this aspect of your digestion and immune functioning. Certain foods labeled "raw" that have been heated slightly for reduction, such as agave and other syrups, will fall into this category (if labeled by a responsible company that understands this standard). Your body will experience no leukocytosis if foods are heated to 200° or less (water boils at 212°).

WHY RAW FOODS?

Any popularity that raw foods have earned over the past forty years has happened simply because they *work*. It will probably take science forty more years to explain all the reasons raw foods are so effective. Regardless, anyone who is interested in raw foods has a reason for being so, and here are the most common of them.

To detox – This is the most common reason people use raw foods – as part of their temporary or seasonal detox programs. This is a great way to keep every system in your body running smoothly, to give it a rest, rejuvenate the digestive system, cleanse the colon, lose a few pounds before summer, etc. Generally, an effective detox period will last from two to four weeks, though it can be shorter if combined with a few days of only fresh juice. Using raw foods in this way is especially helpful for people who feel too overwhelmed by the idea of eating 100% raw foods indefinitely.

To heal – Raw foods have become famous for helping people to self-heal from serious illnesses – in some cases even when Western allopathic medicine has given up on healing the condition. Many people have reported miraculous improvement in their health, especially when following the protocols as taught by educational centers like the Hippocrates Institute and Optimum Health Institute. These protocols do not work for everyone, but they work dramatically for enough people that many of these centers are thriving. A two to three week program at one of these centers is a great way to start, especially if you need personal guidance, or have a digestive weakness or blood sugar condition.

To lose weight – Raw vegan foods are very effective for losing weight, for many reasons: maximum fiber, enzymes for energy, low calories, and pure oils (flax, coconut, olive, avocado) that are easily digested and processed by your liver. When your body stops spending so much energy digesting heavy food, it can spend its energy *eliminating* what's ailing you: body fat, congestion in the lymph, mineral deposits in the joints, and metabolic waste in the blood. This amounts to lower weight, more energy and greater ease of mobility. Allow at least a few days for your body to adjust to the lower calorie intake before exercising too heavily. After all, you want to feel energized and nourished, not drained and hungry.

For greater consciousness – A 100% raw food diet, or a fruit or juice fast, can be an important part of your intention to calm your mind, meditate and pray more often, focus on spirituality, and learn more about your Self. Many spiritual traditions include fasting as a way to feel more in tune with the spiritual dimension, including Buddhism and Catholicism (Lent, the 40-day fast). When you feel better physically, and spend less time preoccupied with highly stimulating foods, the body becomes less of a "distraction,", and your mind and spirit are free to soar. It is also true that on a raw food diet, many people feel that they need less sleep, so they have more time to focus on what's really meaningful in life.

ENZYMES = ENERGY

Living foods come stocked with their own digestive enzymes. When we eat lifeless, enzyme-less foods, our bodies must create digestive enzymes, pulling energy from other areas and organs of the body, which is why eating cooked foods creates a feeling of lethargy, or the feeling that you want to take a nap. Eating raw will help keep your energy naturally elevated.

Conserving the body's enzyme resources is particularly important if you need those resources to heal from a serious illness. For more information, read the classic *Enzyme Nutrition* by Dr. Edward Howell.

BLOOD TYPES AND ALKALINITY

Every health practitioner and nutritionist who works with vegetarians and raw fooders understands the limitations of the eat-for-your-blood-type diet, since people of all blood types have succeeded in healing on raw vegan diets. Far more important than blood type is what all human blood has in common: *it must remain alkaline.*

Natural carnivores have acidic blood and short, smooth colons. Human beings have alkaline blood and long, convoluted colons, like other plant-eaters. Cooked and processed foods and animal products can have an acidic effect on the blood, which in turn causes disease, degeneration and osteoporosis (since your body will leach calcium from your bones to alkalize the blood). So the real question is this: Can you maintain an adequately alkaline pH with the diet you're currently eating? Some meat eaters can, and this may be genetic or related to personality type (stress is acidic).

You can easily test your pH levels using simple paper strips to see if you're too acidic. To alkalize your blood, rely on raw plant foods, especially fresh citrus fruits, leafy greens and almonds. Conversely, the most acidic foods are meats and grains. For more information, read *Become Younger* by Dr. Norman Walker and *Rainbow Green Live Food Cuisine* by Gabriel Cousens, M.D.

BEYOND PROTEIN

The idea that protein comes only from meat and dairy products is a myth. Proteins are basically amino acids, which are present in all raw foods, especially wheatgrass juice, alfalfa sprouts, and sprouted sunflower seeds.

Raw bodybuilders, like Stephen Arlin, author of *Raw Power!: Building Strength and Muscle Naturally*, list these quality sources of protein: heavy greens, like romaine lettuce and kale, as well as avocadoes, olives, coconuts, and flax seeds. See also *On Nutrition and Physical Performance* by Dr. Douglas Graham.

SLOW OR FAST?

The pace at which you'll transition to raw foods will depend on whether you're currently in a health crisis, in which case you'll probably want to transition quickly.

A slow transition is generally more comfortable, and it's a miraculous process listening to our bodies as they change. For more information, I recommend the book *Conscious Eating* by Gabriel Cousens, M.D. The lack of immediate motivation for those of us who are not in emergency situations, however, can be frustrating. It's tempting to put off our commitment to raw foods to a hundred or a thousand tomorrows.

If you want to make a quick transition to raw foods because of immediate health concerns, hold onto your motivation with both hands; read *12 Steps to Raw Foods: How to End Your Addiction to Cooked Food* by Victoria Boutenko; and consider enjoying a retreat at a raw foods healing center, several of which are listed in the back of this book.

Another good book for people facing motivational issues in emergency situations is *Man's Search for Meaning* by Victor Frankl.

HOW RAW IS RAW?

There are many different philosophies of health and spirituality that can pique a person's interest in a raw plant food diet. Each of the health systems listed below encourages a diet consisting of at least 75% raw, living plant foods. Their differences lie in whether they recommend eating any cooked food at all, and if so, what kinds and why.

100% Raw Plant Food Diet - The path to discovering how truly healthy you can be. Devotees enjoy a completely mucusless and alkaline physical state. Books: *The Sunfood Diet Success System* by David Wolfe and *12 Steps to Raw Foods* by Victoria Boutenko.

Hippocrates Diet - A 100% raw plant food diet, focusing on maximum enzyme sources like sprouts, wheatgrass juice and fermented foods like fresh sauerkraut. Books: *The Hippocrates Diet and Health Program* by Dr. Ann Wigmore and *The Living Foods Lifestyle* by Brenda Cobb.

Natural Hygiene - Primarily a raw plant food diet, with cooked complex starches, like potatoes, yams, lentils and legumes, to increase calorie intake. Books: *The Natural Hygiene Handbook* by the American Natural Hygiene Society, and any book by Dr. Herbert M. Shelton.

Essene Diet - Based on *The Essene Gospel of Peace*, God gave us to eat raw seeds, fruit, herbs and milk. That is, milk which is unpasteurized and from healthy animals.

Macrobiotic-Raw Diet - Focus on raw plant foods, with miso, seaweed, and possibly brown rice and cultured soy products included. The focus is on enzymes, and B-complex vitamins. Book: *Dining in the Raw* by Rita Romano.

Hunza Diet - An 80% raw plant food diet with some cooked whole grains and healthy meat and eggs included. A practical approach based on the long-lived, disease-free people of the Hunza culture. Book: *Never Be Sick Again* by Raymond Francis, M.Sc., R.N.C.

Temporary Raw Diet - Raw foods and juices are very effective for purposes of detoxification and colon cleansing. Books: *Cleanse and Purify Thyself* by Richard Anderson and *The Raw Food Detox Diet* by Natalia Rose.

THE SKINNY ON DETOXIFICATION

When we regularly consume processed foods and excess grains, meat and dairy products, our lymphatic systems become overloaded and congested, leaving excess toxins to remain rampant in the blood and in the digestive system where they cause chronic illnesses and diseased colons.

Raw foods help our digestive systems to heal, which allows our lymphatic systems to discharge these congestive toxins. This process can be uncomfortable.

Symptoms of detoxification include a temporary loss of energy, headaches, nausea or diarrhea. Some people will re-experience childhood illnesses. If you experience low energy or bowel irregularities over a long period of time, you may have an overgrowth of yeast or Candida in your intestines.

If eating raw foods makes you feel ill, find a supportive health practitioner who can help you to detox more slowly, and read *The Detox Miracle Sourcebook* by Robert Morse, N.D.

HABITS AND ALLERGIES

As you embark on your own brand of raw diet, be as open as you can be to challenging your previous, habitual tastes. Sweet and salty flavors dominate in the standard American diet, but as Deepak Chopra reminds us, there are six flavors of health: sweet, salty, bitter, pungent, astringent and sour.

Before I'd started eating primarily raw foods, I had disliked avocadoes and olives immensely. Since these are two important raw sources of essential fatty acids, I challenged myself to give each of them another honest try. Lo and behold, I took to raw olives immediately, and I can now say that I miss avocadoes if I go a few days without them. I now even enjoy spicy foods, where I was previously very sensitive to them and disliked peppers in general. Let miracles happen.

Be open to the possibility that your food allergies will change as well. Many people find that as they eat more raw foods and detoxify their bodies, their food allergies, as well as environmental and pet allergies, will disappear. If your allergies are potentially severe or life threatening, however, you may want to work with a health practitioner to determine when you can experiment again with the foods to which you've been allergic.

CONVENIENCE FOODS

Raw-food-to-go is a great timesaving option.

Besides fresh fruit, which is the ultimate convenience food, you can also buy flax seed crackers, raw energy bars and dried fruit at most health food stores now. In some states, you can buy unpasteurized juices in the bottle; for instance, bottled orange and grapefruit juices can legally be sold in California without being pasteurized.

If the stores near you don't carry what you want, you can request them. Fresh salad bars are also convenient and quick, so keep these in mind, including those located in mainstream grocery stores in your area.

If needed, there are companies who can ship convenient raw food items to you. Several are listed in the back of this book.

EATING OUT

Raw restaurants are popping up in cities all over the country and the world, and an increasing number of vegetarian restaurants, and health food stores and delis, are becoming raw food conscious. You can help your local restaurants and delis through the learning curve by turning them on to a few simple raw food recipe books.

In lieu of raw friendly businesses, many mainstream restaurants offer fresh-squeezed orange juice, fruit plates, creative large dinner salads and salad bars, as well as innovative salad dressings. For a healthier salad dressing, you can bring a small bottle of flax oil with you to restaurants and request fresh lemon wedges or fresh chunky salsa. I usually request fresh avocado slices for my salads, which adds some creaminess. In the summertime, some restaurants offer cold, fresh soups, like gazpacho.

Find out where the fresh juice bars are in your area, and include them on your daily route.

Another tactic I use includes bringing my own flax crackers to Mexican restaurants so I can enjoy fresh guacamole and salsa. At Japanese restaurants, I may order miso soup with a green salad. At Jewish delis, I eat fresh pickles and marinated coleslaws and salads.

Once you start looking at the world through "raw eyes," you'll get more creative and feel more comfortable making special requests when you eat out.

CHAPTER 2:
USING THIS BOOK

Over half of the recipes in this book include machine-free options. Some of you may wonder why.

First, machines can be intimidating for raw food beginners. The idea of purchasing and using unfamiliar machinery can be an additional barrier to the already overwhelming project of switching to raw foods.

Secondly, it is unnecessarily time-consuming to assemble, use and clean up after machines.

Thirdly, noisy machinery is contraindicated when one is pursuing a simpler diet and lifestyle.

Therefore, I have structured each chapter as a progression, starting with the simplest recipes, and ending with a recipe that includes a more advanced concept in raw food preparation, like sprouting or using a nut-milk bag.

Each recipe that can be made without a machine will include this symbol:

 = Machine-Free Option

Likewise, if a machine is necessary or optional for a recipe, you will see one or more of these symbols:

For machine-free food preparation, I suggest you have on hand a whisk, a mandoline or manual grater, a manual citrus juicer, and a mortar and pestle if you love pesto. If you're interested in quiet, electricity-free machines, you can purchase a hand crank blender and a manual wheatgrass juicer.

The number one machine I recommend for busy people is a Vita-Mix, since being able to make large batches of smoothies and soups is a real time-saver. The number two machine I recommend is a dehydrator because you can make large batches of convenience foods, suited to your own tastes.

PREPARATION & SERVING SIZES

Preparing raw foods is different from preparing cooked foods, for three main reasons.

First, because we are not sautéing onions, peppers and garlic, etc., to release their flavors. Therefore, we must be patient in letting our foods "marinate" for a little while. It may help to make dishes ahead of time, if possible – for instance, making a party dip the night before you need it.

And second, because the quality of your fresh ingredients and produce is *key*. You can't make a raw marinara sauce taste good without using sweet, vine-ripened tomatoes, for instance. It is common for raw food recipes to taste differently depending on the freshness and ripeness of produce, so if your recipes don't taste good to you, consider this one simple factor. Choose organic and locally grown produce, and ask your local purveyors for advice on how to tell if produce is ripe.

A third way in which raw foods are different has to do with portion planning for meals. Traditional cookbooks are arranged around the entrée-side dish-side dish scenario, where portion sizes are completely standardized. A switch to a raw food diet will often upend the traditional meal planning and cooking habits you've had.

This is primarily because in order to follow the traditional scenario on a raw food diet, you would need to spend a lot of prep time in your kitchen, especially as you learn all new recipes. It is usually far simpler to go the way of most long-time raw fooders and become a "grazer." That is, just make a large batch of a single recipe, or a salad with many toppings, and graze on that until you're satisfied. Or, make a smoothie that fills your blender and sip on it all day.

A related reason is because, after a while of eating raw, it's common to be satisfied with less food.

INGREDIENTS

If some of the ingredients in this book are unfamiliar to you, you can scan the list below for descriptions, including simple tips on how to choose the highest quality ingredients.

Agave nectar: A sweet syrup from a common desert plant.

Bragg's liquid aminos: A healthy salt alternative that is not fermented like soy sauces are.

Carob Powder: A powdered cacao substitute. Choose raw.

Cashews: Buy hand-shelled, truly raw cashews, if possible.

Date sugar: Granulated sugar made from dried dates.

Flax seeds: Small brown or golden seeds, which are high in healthy essential oils. They make great crunchy crackers when dehydrated. Flax oil is great on salads.

Honey: Buy raw, unfiltered honey, and make sure it hasn't been diluted with corn syrup, like many commercial brands are (even though it doesn't say so on the label).

Maca: A powdered nutritious root from Peru that gives a malted flavor to smoothies and beverages.

Maple syrup: Buy the 100% pure variety. Though cooked for reduction, it's the easiest plant-based sweetener to find.

Miso: Miso is a salty, cultured soybean product. Though it's cooked, it's also packed with healthy enzymes.

Nama Shoyu: Unpasteurized soy sauce by Ohsawa.

Oils: Always use cold-pressed, unrefined, organic oils.

Olive Oil: FDA studies show that 96% of the "100% Extra Virgin Olive Oil" bottled in the U.S. is *NOT!* For more information, call or visit the website for Beyond Health.

Olives: Raw olives are those that have not been canned or heat packed in jars.

Salt: Sea salt is rich in minerals. Try Celtic or Himalayan.

Spices: Organic are better. Sun-dried are best.

Tahini: Sesame butter used in popular Middle Eastern dishes like hummus and falafel. Choose raw.

Vinegar: Raw apple cider vinegar is the healthiest unpasteurized, alkalizing vinegar.

Young coconut: Also called a Thai coconut, this is the one covered with tough white fibers. Carefully chop open with a large knife or machete to reach the tender meat and water.

Throughout this book, I often suggest timesaving shortcuts, such as using garlic and ginger powders. However, there is really no substitute for fresh garlic and ginger, when you have the time and energy to prepare it.

If you're avoiding fermented foods, you'll want to substitute fresh lemon juice for vinegar, and Bragg's liquid aminos for Nama Shoyu in these recipes, and you'll want to skip the miso entirely.

WARMING YOUR FOOD

The temperature at which a significant amount of vital enzymes are destroyed in natural foods is somewhere between 108 and 119 degrees.

When warming liquids like soups and sauces, use a double boiler so that the temperature will rise slowly. Stir often, and either use a thermometer or heat just until the liquid is warm to the touch.

When warming entrees, a dehydrator is the safest way to reheat food. About an hour at 105°F, or a little higher, will do. Another option is to use a slightly warmed oven.

Microwaves destroy enzymes, so use sparingly, or never. For further guidance, see *Warming Up to Living Foods* by Elisa Markowitz.

A DAILY MENU

For those of you who aren't sure what a daily raw menu would look like, here's a sample, with plenty of options:

BREAKFAST:
Fresh grapefruit or other fresh fruit, OR
A fruit smoothie or pudding, OR
Hot tea with a Sweet Seed Bar or Nut Butter Cookie

LUNCH:
Small green salad, or coleslaw, WITH
Marinated Vegetables or Waldorf Salad, OR
Pâté or Guacamole with Flax Crackers, OR
Soup or Rellenos or other raw entrée
MID-AFTERNOON:
Fresh vegetable juice, or Jordan's Power Shake

DINNER:
A large green salad, packed with garnishes, olives, avocadoes, sprouts, cucumbers, tomatoes, etc.

EVENING:
A shake, smoothie or fresh fruit, OR
A dessert, energy bar, or cookie

Since our digestive systems are strongest at mid-day, I enjoy my more elaborate recipes then. If your schedule doesn't allow for it, or if you enjoy more creative meals in the evenings, you'll probably want to swap my Lunch suggestions with my Dinner suggestions.

A BUSY WEEK

Here's an example of how a busy person can organize a workweek to support a raw food diet:

SUNDAY:
Make prepared-ahead foods, like a salad dressing and garnish, a pate, a ready-to-use marinade, Ice Dream, a fruit dip, etc.

MONDAY – WEDNESDAY:
Rely on prepared-ahead food items.

THURSDAY – FRIDAY:
Rely on grab-and-go food items, like fresh fruit, oil and vinegar for your salads, Guacamole, smoothies and quick soups.

SATURDAY:
Take some time to prepare and enjoy gourmet recipes, like Rellenos, Cottage Pie, Nori Rolls, Refried Almonds, etc.

ONE SUNDAY PER MONTH:
Stack your dehydrator with foods you can enjoy all month.

KITCHEN GADGETS

Whisk: The whisk is a busy person's best friend for easy clean-up and no noise. Get some in various sizes.

Mandoline: It works fast, keeps your fingers safe, and washes off faster than a food processor.

Saladacco: Great for creating pastas from zucchini and butternut squash, and beautiful beet garnishes for your salads. See Appendix I.

Whisk

Mortar & Pestle: The old-fashioned, machine-free way to mash green herbs, garlic cloves and pine nuts to make pesto. Made of stone or wood.

Sharp Knives Ceramic knives make food prep a breeze.

Seed or Cofee Grinder: Use to grind seeds and spices, and dried zests, garlic and ginger.

Blender: A VitaMix or heavy duty blender will create smoother sauces, soups and pates. Thicker recipes made in a regular kitchen blender may require more water or liquid to be added.

Citrus Juicer: A manual one will do quite well for simple recipes and single juice servings.

Mortar & pestle

Mandoline slicer

Manual citrus juicer

RECIPES

Raw Foods for Busy People

CHAPTER 3:
EXCITING SALADS

Green salads and fresh fruit form a strong dietary base for us humans. However, for the vast majority of us, our palates have received constant stimulation from such a wide variety of cooked foods that the switch to eating a large green salad or two every day can take some getting used to. It can seem boring, or repetitive, at first. That is, until the sigh of relief your body gives you every time you eat raw fruits and greens overpowers that desire for the cooked, processed foods of yore.

Well, it's time for greener pastures! This chapter lists some exciting ways to turn your green salads into fields of adventure. If you make a week's worth of a different raw salad dressing and salad garnish each weekend, you'll find yourself looking forward to your salads every day of the week.

Making your own salad dressings will help you to avoid refined sugars, acidic vinegars and processed oils. Of course, simple flaxseed or olive oil, with raw apple cider vinegar or fresh lemon juice, makes the most effortless salad dressing.

Recipes for coleslaws and Waldorf salad are also included in this chapter, as is a brief introduction to sprouting techniques.

For fruit salad dressings, please see page 67 in the "Dip This, Dip That" chapter, and page 85 in the "Desserts, Snacks & Shakes" chapter.

⊘ Ⓑ SIMPLE VINAIGRETTES

Keep this one handy. It makes a great marinade too.

BASIC VINAIGRETTE:

1 cup cold-pressed olive oil

½ cup raw cider or balsamic vinegar, or a mixture

3 cloves garlic, minced, or ½ tsp. garlic powder

2 Tbsp pure honey or agave syrup

1 tsp each sea salt and black pepper

2 tsp each dried oregano and basil

Dried chili peppers (optional)

CREAMY VINAIGRETTE:

Add 3-4 stalks of celery to the Basic Vinaigrette recipe

RASPBERRY VINAIGRETTE:

½ Basic Vinaigrette recipe

1 pint raspberries, fresh or frozen

½ cup fresh orange juice

1 chopped scallion

MARINATED MUSHROOMS OR CHERRY TOMATOES:

Mushrooms or tomatoes, plus Basic Vinaigrette to coat

A Basic Vinaigrette can be assembled in any kind of a jar, and then shaken before each use. For the Raspberry or Creamy Vinaigrette, use a blender.

Marinate cherry tomatoes or mushrooms, or any other vegetable of your choice, in the Basic Vinaigrette for 30-60 minutes at room temperature, stirring often, or overnight in the refrigerator, stirring occasionally. Enjoy as a salad garnish, or as munchies at any time of day.

⊘ GRAPEFRUIT DRESSING

Add pea pods and mung bean sprouts for an exotic salad.

2/3 cup fresh grapefruit juice

2 Tbsp cold-pressed olive oil

1 Tbsp raw cider vinegar

1 Tbsp agave syrup or honey

¼ cup red onion, minced

2 Tbsp finely chopped cilantro

Pinch of sea salt and black pepper

Combine all ingredients and toss with mixed greens.

⊘ ⓑ TAHINI DRESSING

Tahini makes a deliciously rich dressing for salads.

2/3 cup raw sesame tahini

1 cup water

¼ cup fresh lemon or orange juice

1 clove garlic, minced, or ¼ tsp. garlic powder

¼ cup chopped parsley

1 tsp sea salt and a pinch of cayenne

1 pitted date (optional)

BELL PEPPER SALAD:

2 cups diced bell peppers, mixed colors

1 cup chopped cauliflower

½ cup chopped red onion

1 stalk celery, chopped

1/3 cup Tahini Dressing

1 Tbsp Italian Seasoning

Use a whisk to mix the dressing, or for a super smooth dressing, use a blender.
For the Bell Pepper Salad, simply toss and serve.

⊘ Ⓑ INSTANT RANCH DRESSING

You can whip this up in two minutes flat.

1 cup raw cashew butter

½ cup water

3 Tbsp fresh lemon juice

1 tsp raw cider vinegar

Pinch of salt

1 tsp Italian seasoning or dried dill

1 clove garlic, or 1/8 tsp garlic powder

1 stalk celery

Combine all ingredients in a blender and whip until smooth and creamy.
For a machine-free version, replace the salt and celery stalk with a bit of celery salt, and make sure your cashew butter is at room temperature.

⊘ Ⓑ AVOCADO DRESSING

Creates a salad packed with essential oils.

2 ripe avocadoes

3-4 Tbsp fresh lemon juice

1 clove garlic

1 medium cucumber, peeled

¼ cup chopped scallions OR red onion

1 Tbsp Italian seasoning OR dried dill

AVOCADO TOMATO DRESSING:

Add 1 ripe tomato

Blend all ingredients together, adding water to desired consistency.

Avocadoes can easily be whipped to a creamy and smooth consistency without a blender, so if you use a whisk, simply replace the cucumber with enough water to thin.

Ⓑ NATURE'S WISDOM DRESSING

The famous, rich and tasty dressing.

1/3 cup raw cider vinegar

¼ cup Nama Shoyu, wheat-free tamari or liquid aminos

½ cup raspberries or mixed berries, fresh or frozen

½ large avocado

½ medium onion, chopped

A few chunks of pineapple, fresh or frozen

1 clove garlic or 1/8 tsp garlic powder

1 tsp black pepper

1-2 Tbsp agave syrup or honey (optional)

½ cup cold-pressed olive oil

Blend all ingredients except olive oil and blend well. Add olive oil, pulse blend, and serve.

⊘ JORDAN'S SLACKER SALAD

This is my dinner when I feel really lazy.

1 chopped ripe tomato

1 handful of fresh olives

1 chopped avocado (optional)

Basic Vinaigrette Dressing (page 29)

Toss and enjoy.

⊘ COOL MINT SALAD

Cool, light and refreshing, all year round.

1 cup chopped cucumbers

1 cup chopped ripe tomatoes

1/3 cup chopped fresh mint

¼ cup chopped parsley

2 Tbsp fresh lemon juice

1 Tbsp cold-pressed olive oil

¼ cup sprouted sunflower seeds (page 40) (optional)

RAWESOME TABOULI:

Increase chopped parsley to 1 cup

Add ½ recipe Sprouted Lentil Salad (page 40) minus vinegar

Toss all ingredients and allow to marinate in the refrigerator at least one hour, stirring often.

GREEK SALAD

A taste of the Mediterranean at home.

1 large ripe tomato, diced

1 large cucumber, seeded and sliced

½ large red onion, halved and sliced

½ cup kalamata olives, whole or sliced

1 medium beet, quartered and finely sliced (optional)

3 Tbsp cold-pressed olive oil

2 Tbsp fresh lemon juice

1 Tbsp raw cider vinegar

½ tsp each dried oregano and basil

Pinch of garlic powder, sea salt and black pepper

Combine all ingredients, marinate for at least 30 minutes, and serve on a bed of romaine lettuce and spinach. *Opa!*

CHINESE CELERY SALAD

A taste of the Orient.

6 stalks celery, thinly sliced

1 cup sliced mushrooms of your choice

2 Tbsp Nama Shoyu or wheat-free tamari

1 Tbsp raw cider vinegar

1 Tbsp unrefined sesame oil

1 tsp fresh grated ginger, or ¼ tsp. ginger powder

Pinch of salt

Bed of sliced Chinese cabbage and shredded carrots

Toss all ingredients except cabbage and carrots and marinate for at least 30 minutes. Serve over Chinese cabbage and carrots.

Raw Foods for Busy People

⊘ CAULIFLOWER ORANGE SALAD

The best recipe I ever translated from Betty Crocker.

½ small head of cauliflower, chopped

½ bell pepper, chopped

½ cup chopped green beans or broccoli

1 ½ cups mandarin orange segments

3 Tbsp fresh lemon juice

3 Tbsp cold-pressed flaxseed or olive oil

1 tsp pure maple syrup or honey

½ tsp orange zest

Salt and black pepper to taste

Serve on a bed of spinach, and garnish with chives

Toss all ingredients and marinate for two to three hours at room temperature, stirring often, or overnight in the refrigerator, stirring occasionally.

For a more portable version, skip the green beans or broccoli, and add 1-2 cups of chopped spinach, allowing it to marinate and reduce within the salad.

⊘ Ⓕ LIGHT SUMMER COLE SLAW

Click your heels three times, and you'll have it memorized.

3 cups shredded green and/or red cabbage

1 cup shredded carrots

2 celery stalks, thinly sliced

2 Tbsp chopped parsley

½ cup raw pecans or walnuts, or nuts of your choice

¼ cup unrefined sesame oil

2 Tbsp raw cider vinegar

½ tsp garlic powder

½ cup sun-dried tomatoes, soaked 15 minutes, chopped (optional)

1 tsp fennel or poppy seeds (optional)

Salt and black pepper to taste

Slice the cabbage and carrots by hand, or use a mandoline o food processor. Toss all ingredients and marinate for at least on hour, stirring often.

⊘ SWEET RED CABBAGE

Kids of all ages will love this.

4 cups red cabbage, thinly sliced

2 pears or apples, sliced

3 green onions, sliced

1 carrot, grated

½ cup raisins or currants

4 Tbsp sweet apple juice, or 2Tbsp agave syrup

3 Tbsp cold-pressed olive oil

1 Tbsp raw cider vinegar

½ tsp dry mustard (optional)

Salt and pepper to taste

Toss all ingredients together and marinate for at least one hour at room temperature, stirring often.

⊘ Ⓑ Ⓕ CREAMY PINEAPPLE SALADS

A sweet, tropical treat.

CREAMY PINEAPPLE SAUCE:

¼ cup raw cashew or macadamia butter

¼ cup pineapple juice OR 1/3 cup chopped pineapple

1 Tbsp fresh lemon juice

½ Tbsp cold-pressed olive oil

2 tsp dried dill

CREAMY PINEAPPLE COLESLAW:

2 cups shredded green cabbage

½ cup shredded carrots

1 cup pineapple chunks

2 Tbsp chopped parsley

Creamy Pineapple Sauce

Salt and pepper to taste

PINEAPPLE WALDORF SALAD:

1 chopped apple

½ cup pineapple chunks

3 stalks celery, sliced

3-4 scallions, chopped

½ cup raw walnuts or pecans

¼ cup parsley, chopped

Creamy Pineapple Sauce

Salt to taste

Whisk or blend sauce ingredients together. If using a whisk, make sure the nut butter is at room temperature. If using a blender, add the dill last and gently pulse blend. For very fine coleslaw, you can shred the cabbage with a food processor.

Toss all ingredients, and serve fresh. Waldorf Salad is great served on a bed of leafy greens.

⊘ BROCCOLI WALNUT SALAD

A hearty favorite all year round.

1 large bunch broccoli, chopped

½ cup shredded carrots

2 Tbsp raw cider vinegar

2 Tbsp pure maple syrup or agave syrup

3 Tbsp cold-pressed flax or unrefined sesame oil

¼ tsp dry mustard

¼ cup chopped raw walnuts

Whisk together the vinegar, syrup, oil and mustard. Toss with the broccoli and carrots, and serve immediately or marinate for one hour, stirring often, to soften the broccoli somewhat. Top with chopped walnuts before serving.

⊘ Ⓑ TAHINI WALDORF SALAD

An excellent dish to take to a potluck.

1 red apple, chopped

1 firm pear or green apple, chopped

1 cup red grapes, cut in half

4 celery stalks, sliced

3 scallions, chopped

1/3 cup raisins

1/3 cup walnuts, pecans or almonds, chopped or sliced

Fresh parsley or mint to garnish

DRESSING:

¼ cup raw sesame tahini

1/3 cup water or apple juice

1/3 cup fresh lemon juice (reduce to ¼ cup if using apple juice)

3 Tbsp raw cider vinegar

2 Tbsp pure honey or agave syrup

1 Tbsp cold-pressed flax or unrefined sesame oil

1 tsp sea salt or a dash of liquid aminos or tamari

Whisk or blend the dressing ingredients together, then toss with the rest of the ingredients.

Serve on a bed of lettuce, if desired.

⊘ Ⓕ FESTIVE SALAD GARNISHES

These are great topped with avocado slices.

4 cups shredded carrots, beets and/or Daikon radish

¼ cup each minced scallions and parsley

One of the marinades from Chapter 4, OR

Sour Cream (page 48), OR

TANGY MARINADE:

¼ cup fresh orange juice

2 Tbsp fresh lemon juice

1 Tbsp cold-pressed olive oil

1 Tbsp orange zest

Pinch of cayenne

It's easiest to make a week's worth of these salad garnishes by using the shredding blade on a food processor, but a mandoline or hand shredder will work just as well.

Toss all ingredients and marinate for 30-60 minutes, stirring often.

Serve as a garnish with a green salad.

⊘ SPROUTS DEMYSTIFIED

The trick is in the timing.

1 cup seeds or legumes soaked in 4 cups water

SUNFLOWER SEEDS: Soak 8-12 hours, air dry for 2-4 hours
GARBANZOS/LENTILS: Soak 8-12 hours, air dry 2-3 days

Sprouting is easy, in concept. The challenge for busy people is to remember that something's sprouting, and to drain or rinse the seeds or legumes in a timely manner.

Soak your seeds or legumes in the refrigerator overnight, then rinse well. Leave them in the strainer or colander to allow them to air dry, re-rinsing the legumes once per day. Legumes will be ready to use when they sprout a tail about ¼ inch long.

Sprouted seeds and legumes are great on green salads. Use sunflower seeds for making Versatile Pates (page 70), or use lentils in the Sprouted Lentil Salad (below).

⊘ SPROUTED LENTIL SALAD

Use plenty of tomato, and serve with a green salad.

1 ½ cups sprouted lentils

1 ½ cups chopped ripe tomatoes

½ cup each chopped onion and bell pepper

2 Tbsp fresh lemon juice or raw cider vinegar

4 Tbsp cold-pressed olive oil

1 tsp pure honey or maple syrup

Sea salt to taste

Toss sprouted lentils with the rest of the ingredients, and allow to marinate at least one hour.

Serve as a garnish with a green salad, or use in the Rawsome Tabouli recipe on page 33.

CHAPTER 4:
MARINADES AND OTHER WET STUFF

These recipes are my favorites because they punctuate the ease and simplicity of raw foods. Chop up a batch of your favorite veggies, add a marinade, and munch on them for days.

Here's the easiest way to marinate: Simply seal your vegetables and marinade of choice in an air-tight container; leave it on your counter for a few hours; and shake it up whenever you walk by. Or, if you leave the container in your refrigerator, you can give it a shake when you go in there for something else.

Another bonus: when you use marinades that include acidic ingredients, like lemon juice, Nama Shoyu, or cider vinegar, the vegetables will soften as they "simmer" in the marinade. This is true especially of mushrooms, broccoli, and greens like spinach or bok choy.

Most of these recipes can be made without machinery, so the clean up is almost nil. Remember your whisk? Dust it off, honey!

⊘ SIMPLEST MARINADES

Memorize it. Use it. Play with it!

3 Tbsp Nama Shoyu or wheat-free tamari

1-2 cloves garlic

1 Tbsp fresh lime or lemon juice

1 tsp pure honey or agave syrup

Black pepper or cayenne

1 Tbsp unrefined sesame or cold-pressed olive oil

POLYNESIAN MARINADE:

Use fresh pineapple juice and chunks in place of citrus

MEDITERRANEAN MARINADE:

Omit Nama Shoyu or tamari

Increase olive oil to ¼ cup and lemon juice to 3 Tbsp

Add 1 tsp oregano, and chopped olives to taste

MISO MARINADE:

Reduce Nama Shoyu or tamari to 1 Tbsp

Increase oil to 2 Tbsp

Add 1 Tbsp unpasteurized miso

Whisk ingredients together. Marinate vegetables of your choice for one hour at room temperature, stirring often, or overnight in the refrigerator, stirring occasionally.

Serve atop fresh, crunchy bean sprouts, or make Vegetable Kabobs (page 76).

⊘ Ⓑ ALMOND BUTTER MARINADE

You can make this rich sauce as spicy as you like.

½ cup each raw almond butter and water

¼ cup Nama Shoyu, wheat-free tamari or liquid aminos

¼ cup pure honey, or chopped dates

3-4 cloves garlic

1 tsp raw cider vinegar

Crushed red pepper, cayenne, and sea salt to taste

Whisk or blend all ingredients together. Toss with vegetables of your choice and marinate for at least 30 minutes at room temperature, stirring often, or overnight in the refrigerator, stirring occasionally.
   If using dates, you'll want to use a blender.
   Serve as is, or atop fresh, crunchy bean sprouts.

⊘ MOROCCAN MARINADE

A blend of exotic flavors.

¼ cup cold-pressed olive or unrefined sesame oil

3 tsp coriander

1 ½ tsp cinnamon

2 Tbsp fresh lemon juice

2 tsp pure honey or agave syrup (optional)

1 tsp dried orange peel or saffron (optional)

Whisk the marinade and toss with vegetables of your choice. Marinate for at least 30 minutes at room temperature, stirring often, or overnight in the refrigerator, stirring occasionally.
   I suggest including fresh chopped tomatoes and bell peppers when using this sauce. It's also a good marinade for shredded yam.

⊘ CURRIED APPLE MARINADE

This sauce is great with carrots, cauliflower and bell peppers.

½ cup apple juice, preferably fresh

2 Tbsp unrefined sesame or cold-pressed olive oil

2-4 Tbsp diced onion

1 tsp garam masala or curry powder

¼ tsp each dry mustard and black pepper

Cayenne to taste, or minced hot peppers

Combine all ingredients. Toss with vegetables and marinate for at least 30 minutes, stirring often, or overnight in the refrigerator, stirring occasionally.

Serve atop fresh, crunchy bean sprouts, or make Vegetable Kabobs (page 76).

⊘ SZECHWAN MARINADE

This is a powerful sauce best made with rice wine.

¼ cup unrefined sesame oil

2-3 Tbsp rice wine

2-3 Tbsp Nama Shoyu or wheat-free tamari

3 cloves garlic, or ½ tsp garlic powder

1 tsp dry mustard

½ tsp crushed red pepper, or minced hot peppers

Whisk the ingredients together and toss with vegetables of your choice. Marinate for at least 30 minutes at room temperature, stirring often, or overnight in the refrigerator, stirring occasionally.

Serve atop fresh, crunchy bean sprouts, or make Vegetable Kabobs (page 76).

Ⓑ MARINARA MARINADE

Try chopped zucchini, bell peppers and mushrooms with this sauce.

2 large ripe tomatoes

2 Tbsp cold-pressed olive oil

1 tsp raw cider vinegar or fresh lemon juice

2 Tbsp Italian Seasoning

1 small clove garlic

2-4 black olives, chopped (optional)

½ Tbsp sweetener of choice (optional)

Salt to taste

PIZZA SAUCE: Add ½ cup sun-dried tomatoes, soaked 15 minutes

SPAGHETTI: Serve Marinara Marinade over zucchini noodles

Blend all ingredients and toss with vegetables of your choice. Marinate for at least 30 minutes at room temperature, stirring often, or overnight in the refrigerator, stirring occasionally.

To make zucchini noodles, use a Saladacco or Spirooli spiralizer. The noodles can be warmed in a dehydrator for 30 minutes, or in a double boiler with the sauce, just until warm.

Add sun-dried tomatoes for a smoother, richer sauce. Use as a pizza spread, with Italian Flax Crackers you can purchase or dehydrate yourself (page 78).

LIVE SPAGHETTI:

Enjoy live, gluten-free pasta made from zucchini and butternut squash! Cut zucchini into the shapes of angel hair, thick spaghetti and fettucine, using a simple garnishing machine. See Appendix I for details.

⊘ CITRUS GINGER MARINADE

Fresh ginger makes this sauce exquisite.

½ cup fresh orange or pineapple juice

¼ cup Nama Shoyu or wheat-free tamari

1 Tbsp fresh grated ginger

2-3 cloves garlic, or ½ tsp garlic powder

1-2 Tbsp pure honey or agave syrup

1 Tbsp unrefined sesame oil

Whisk or shake the ingredients together and toss with vegetables of your choice. Marinate for at least 30 minutes at room temperature, stirring often, or overnight in the refrigerator, stirring occasionally.

Serve atop fresh, crunchy bean sprouts; dehydrate for Vegetable Kabobs (page 76); or use to make Asian Pate (page 70).

⊘ Ⓑ MIDDLE EASTERN MARINADE

Include diced zucchini and ripe tomato for a rich, flavorful dish.

2/3 cup raw sesame tahini

1 cup water

3 Tbsp fresh lemon juice

2 cloves garlic, minced, or ¼ tsp. garlic powder

¼ cup chopped parsley

1 tsp cumin

½ tsp each sea salt and black pepper

Use a whisk to mix the marinade, or use a blender to make it super smooth. Marinate vegetables for at least 30 minutes, stirring often.

Ⓑ SOUR CREAM

A creamy classic with a smooth consistency.

1 cup raw cashews, soaked 30 minutes and drained

¼ cup fresh lemon juice

½ stalk celery, peeled and chopped

Pinch of sea salt

1 scallion, chopped, to garnish (optional)

Blend cashews with lemon juice and a little water, if needed, until really smooth. Scrape the sides of the blender with a spatula to aid in blending. Add the remaining ingredients.

Use to accompany Anything-You-Want Borscht (page 59), or Rawsome Rellenos (page 80).

Ⓑ PINEAPPLE BARBECUE SAUCE

Fresh and tangy. Accept no substitute.

1 cup chopped ripe tomatoes

½ cup sun-dried tomatoes, soaked 15 minutes, chopped

1/3 cup pineapple chunks

¼ cup chopped onion

1 small clove garlic, or 1/8 tsp. garlic powder

¼ tsp cayenne, or minced hot peppers

2 Tbsp pure maple syrup, or to taste

3 Tbsp cold-pressed olive or unrefined sesame oil

1 tsp sea salt, or to taste

¼ tsp each paprika and black pepper

Combine all ingredients, and blend until smooth.

Use to top off a batch of Vegetable Kabobs (page 76), or the Barbecue Portobello (next page). It's also used as the base for Chunky Tomato Chili (page 58).

⊘ Ⓑ BARBECUE PORTOBELLO

A hearty meal you can create to suit your tastes.

Vegetable Kabobs, made with chunks of Portobello (page 76)

Pineapple Barbecue Sauce (previous page)

Crispy Onion Toppers (page 76)

For a satisfying entrée, drizzle the Kabobs with Pineapple Barbecue Sauce, and garnish with Crispy Onion Toppers. For a machine-free version, simply toss marinated vegetables and Portobello with fresh chopped tomato and pineapple chunks, and drizzle with a little maple syrup.

⊘ Ⓑ QUICKEST GRAVY

So simple, you'll wonder where it's been all your life.

¾ cup water

1 Tbsp unpasteurized miso

2 Tbsp raw almond butter or sesame tahini

1/8 tsp garlic powder

Pinch of black pepper

Whisk or blend all ingredients together.
Use over Vegetable Kabobs (p. 76) or instead of the Barbecue Sauce on the Barbecue Portobello (above). Or, pour it over a batch of the "Mashed Potatoes" that form the topping of the Cottage Pie (next page).

Ⓕ COTTAGE PIE

The Queen Mother never had it so good!

2 cups total chopped broccoli, cauliflower and carrots

½ cup minced celery

¼ cup minced red onion

¼ cup chopped parsley

2 Tbsp cold-pressed olive oil

2 Tbsp Nama Shoyu, wheat-free tamari or liquid aminos

½ Tbsp organic red wine (optional)

1 clove garlic, minced, or ¼ tsp. garlic powder

Pinch of black pepper or cayenne

¼ cup sun-dried tomatoes, soaked 15 minutes, chopped

"MASHED POTATOES":

2 cups chopped cauliflower

2/3 cup raw cashews or macadamias, soaked 30 min.

¼ cup fresh lemon juice

2 Tbsp cold-pressed olive oil

1 clove garlic, or ¼ tsp garlic powder

1 tsp rosemary or Italian Seasoning

Sea salt and black pepper to taste

Marinate vegetables in olive oil, Nama Shoyu, wine, garlic and black pepper for at least 1 hour, or overnight. For a smoother sauce, blend the marinade liquids with the sun-dried tomatoes and re-toss with the vegetables, before assembling the pies.

To make the "mashed potatoes", grind the nuts in a food processor, then add the cauliflower and the rest of the ingredients. Process until smooth.

Assemble the pies in individual tins, or layered in small bowls, with the "mashed potatoes" on top of the marinated vegetables. Allow the ingredients to reach room temperature, or heat in a warm oven for 1 hour, before serving. Garnish with paprika.

CHAPTER 5:
SUPER SIMPLE
SOUPS

Raw soups are super flavorful, and they can easily be warmed.

To warm a raw soup, use a double boiler so the temperature will rise slowly. Stirring often, warm the soup until it reaches no more than 119°F on a thermometer, or until it is warm to the touch.

I like making raw soups because they're fast, and generally easy to memorize. There are soups for every mood and occasion, from light cucumber soups to rich almond soups. Some, like Borscht and Chunky Tomato Chili, simply beg for creativity.

Once you try all the soups in this section, you'll be really good friends with your blender!

⊘ MISO ALMOND SOUP

A quick enzyme boost, and easy to memorize.

1 Tbsp unpasteurized miso

½ Tbsp raw almond butter

1 cup warm or hot water

¼ cup finely chopped vegetables, mushrooms or nori (optional)

½ chopped scallion to garnish

The vegetables will soften if you allow them to steep in hot water before stirring in the miso and nut butter.

⊘ Ⓑ RICH ALMOND SOUP

These are best warmed, and served with a light salad.

¼ cup raw almond butter

1 cup water

2 Tbsp fresh lemon or orange juice

1 Tbsp Nama Shoyu or wheat-free tamari

2 Tbsp pure honey or agave syrup, or 3 pitted dates

2 scallions, minced

Cayenne, or chopped hot peppers, to taste

NUTTY BROCCOLI OR CAULIFLOWER SOUP:

Add 2 cups chopped broccoli or cauliflower

Omit sweetener, and add ½ tsp curry powder or cumin

If you're using a whisk to make this soup, make sure the almond butter is at room temperature. If you're using dates, or the broccoli or cauliflower, use a blender or VitaMix.

CREAMY AVOCADO SOUP

Avocado = Smooth + Satisfying

2 large ripe avocadoes

½ cup water

3 Tbsp fresh lemon juice

1 clove garlic, or ¼ tsp garlic powder

Sea salt, or liquid aminos, to taste

2 Tbsp Italian Seasoning

CITRUS SOUP: Add 1 cup orange juice + 1 tsp minced jalapeno
MEXICAN SOUP: Omit Italian Seasoning; add ½ tsp each cumin and black pepper, 1 tsp minced jalapeno and 2 Tbsp minced red onion
GREEN SOUP: Add 1 ½ cup chopped spinach OR broccoli

Combine all ingredients, and whisk or blend until smooth. If adding broccoli, use a blender.

COOL CUCUMBER SOUP

This crisp, refreshing soup will soothe your digestion.

2 large cucumbers, peeled, seeded and chopped

¼ cup fresh lemon juice

1 tsp sea salt, or to taste

Water to thin

2 Tbsp raw sesame tahini, or 1 avocado (optional)

1 scallion, chopped

¼ cup fresh mint or dill

Combine all except the scallions and herbs, and whip until smooth. Add the scallions and herbs and pulse blend, leaving the greens in small pieces.

⊘ Ⓑ TANGY FRUIT SOUPS

Any fruit can be used for soup, with a bit of fresh mint.
Add nut butter or tahini for a richer base.

EZ FRUIT SOUP:

½ cup apple juice OR 1 whole apple, chopped

1-2 cups fresh orange juice

¼ cup chopped fresh mint

Chopped hot peppers to taste (optional)

2 Tbsp raw sesame tahini, almond or cashew butter (optional)

REAL FRUIT SOUP:

Add 2 cups fruit of your choice to EZ Fruit Soup

WALDORF SOUP:

Use 2 Tbsp raw cashew butter or sesame tahini with EZ Fruit Soup

Add 2 Tbsp pure honey or 3 soft dates

Add 2 stalks of celery

Add ¼ cup each chopped parsley and scallions

FRUIT-FOR-DINNER SOUP:

Add 1 cup fresh carrot/celery/beet/pepper juice to EZ Fruit Soup

Add 1 fresh tomato, diced, and salt to taste

Blend or whisk the tahini or nut butters first, with the juice, before adding the rest of the ingredients. If using a whisk, it's best if your nut butters and juices are at room temperature. Float pieces of the fruit of your choice, or whole berries, in the soup. If using hot peppers, add conservatively and allow to marinate at least one hour in the refrigerator before adding more.

Garnish with fresh mint.

⊘ Ⓑ WATERMELON BISQUE

Refreshing and tasty at any time of the day.

2 cups ripe watermelon chunks, seeded

1 medium ripe tomato, finely chopped

1 small cucumber, peeled, seeded and finely chopped

2 Tbsp finely chopped cilantro

1 small scallion, minced

2 Tbsp fresh lime or lemon juice

¼ tsp sea salt

½ small jalapeno, minced (optional)

Mash watermelon chunks well and combine all ingredients. You can also blend some of the watermelon with the cucumber in a blender, if desired.

Ⓑ MANGO MINT SOUP

This is your summer coolant.

8 oz mango chunks, fresh or frozen

1 large cucumber, peeled

1 cup fresh orange juice

¼ cup chopped red onion

1 Tbsp pure agave syrup or honey

Pinch of cayenne (optional)

12 to 15 leaves fresh mint

CREAMY MANGO SOUP: Add 1 ripe avocado

Blend all ingredients, adding the fresh mint last.

⊘ SPINACH MUSHROOM SOUP

Rich and warm-feeling, even when it's cold.

¼ cup minced red onion

1 clove garlic, or 1/8 tsp garlic powder

1 Tbsp fresh lemon juice

1 Tbsp Nama Shoyu or wheat-free tamari

½ Tbsp cold-pressed olive or unrefined sesame oil

½ tsp nutmeg

¼ tsp dried mustard

1 cup packed, finely chopped spinach

¾ cup small, thinly sliced mushrooms

2 Tbsp raw sesame tahini

2 Tbsp unpasteurized miso

2 cups water

Marinate the onion, garlic, lemon juice, tamari, olive oil and spices for about 30 minutes, then add the spinach and mushrooms and marinate for 1-2 hours more, stirring often. In a separate bowl, whisk together the tahini, miso and water, then combine all ingredients and stir well.

If desired, heat in a double boiler until lukewarm.

ⓑ FRESH TOMATO SOUPS

Use organic, ripe tomatoes. These recipes build on each other, so you can stay simple, or get crazy.

REAL TOMATO SOUP:

4 medium ripe tomatoes

1 stalk celery

½ bell pepper, chopped

2 Tbsp fresh basil, or 1 tsp Italian Seasoning

2 tsp fresh lemon juice

Salt, cayenne, and minced hot peppers to taste

CREAM OF TOMATO SOUP:

Add 1 ripe avocado, and 2 tsp pure maple or agave syrup

GO-GO GAZPACHO:

Blend a dash of raw cider vinegar with the Real Tomato Soup

Stir in minced zucchini, bell peppers and parsley

CHUNKY TOMATO CHILI:

Blend 1 cup BBQ Sauce (page 48) with the Real Tomato Soup

Blend in 2 tsp chili powder, or hot peppers to taste

Mix in chunks of zucchini, bell peppers and green beans

Combine all ingredients of the Real Tomato Soup in a blender, and puree until desired consistency.

For the Cream of Tomato, Gazpacho, or Chili, blend the avocado and syrup, the vinegar, or the Barbecue Sauce and chili powder, respectively, with the Basic Tomato Soup recipe, and mix in the chopped vegetables by hand, where indicated.

⊘ Ⓑ BORSCHT

From traditional to modern, this is a sweet favorite the world over.

JUICE BAR BORSCHT:

2 cups fresh beet/carrot/celery/red pepper juice

2 Tbsp raw sesame tahini

½ Tbsp fresh lemon juice

½ Tbsp Nama Shoyu, tamari or aminos

Chopped scallions

Finely chopped cabbage

Sea salt and black pepper to taste

ANYTHING-YOU-WANT BORSCHT:

Juice Bar Borscht base

1 cup grated beets

1 red pepper or hot peppers, chopped

½ tsp paprika

Chopped scallions

Chopped red or green cabbage

Chopped carrots

Sliced celery

Chopped apple

Diced avocado

Dollop of Sour Cream (page 48)

For Juice Bar Borscht, simply purchase fresh vegetable juice and whisk all ingredients together except scallions and cabbage. Float scallions and cabbage in the soup.

For Anything-You-Want Borscht, simply add grated beets, peppers and paprika to the Juice Bar Borscht base, and blend until smooth. Float any of the other ingredients (or any others you can think of!) in the soup.

ⓑ FRESH CORN CHOWDER

I never knew corn didn't need to be cooked!

2 cups fresh corn, cut from the cob

1 cup water

¼ cup raw almond or cashew butter or sesame tahini

2 scallions, minced

½ tsp cumin OR pumpkin pie spice

Salt and pepper to taste

Minced red pepper to garnish

Chopped cilantro or sprouts to garnish

Blend the corn, water, nut butter or tahini, scallions and spice until smooth. Add salt and pepper to taste, and garnish with minced red pepper, and chopped cilantro or sprouts. This soup is great warmed (see page 51).

ⓑ CURRIED COCONUT SOUP

This soup is well worth tackling a young coconut.

Meat and water from one young coconut

3 cups shredded carrots OR butternut squash

1 medium chopped onion

1 Tbsp fresh lemon, lime or orange juice

1-2 Tbsp curry powder

1 tsp ground ginger

Pinch of cayenne, or minced hot peppers

Chopped cilantro to garnish

Blend all ingredients except the cilantro.
Add cilantro just before serving.

CHAPTER 6:
DIP THIS,
DIP THAT

Dips are fun, there's no doubt about it. They are commonly a party food, are they not? From guacamole to salsas, nut spreads, garlicky pates, and fruit dips, these versatile dishes will give you that party feeling any day of the week. Furthermore, they're nutritious. Avocadoes, nuts and sprouted seeds are a great way to get high-quality protein and essential oils in your diet.

I have also included Nori Rolls in this chapter, which you can fill with the EZ Nori Filling (page 69), or with a Versatile Sunflower Pate (page 70).

So, go ahead! Dip vegetables, dip fruit, dip flax crackers and carrot chips. Throw yourself a party!

⊘ AVOCADO STRAIGHT UP

Take advantage of the natural creaminess of avocado.

1 ripe avocado

½ lemon or lime

Sea salt and black pepper or cayenne

Carrot sticks or Flax Crackers

Cut an avocado in half, and remove the pit. Squeeze fresh lemon or lime juice over each half, and season with a dash of salt and pepper or cayenne. Use carrot sticks or Flax Crackers (page 78) to scoop the avocado right out of the skin.

⊘ⓓ QUICK AVOCADO PIZZA

Rich and nutritious, even when you're in a rush.

1 ripe avocado

Italian Seasoning

Italian or garlic-flavored Flax Crackers (page 78)

Chopped olives, onion, peppers, zucchini, and mushrooms

Spread fresh avocado on Flax Crackers you've bought or dehydrated yourself, sprinkle with Italian Seasoning, and top with veggies of your choice. *Voila!*

⊘ KITCHEN SINK GUACAMOLE

Perfect whether you only have a few minutes to whip something up, or you really want to show off.

2 ripe avocadoes

2-3 Tbsp fresh lemon or lime juice

1-2 cloves garlic, minced, or ¼ tsp. garlic powder

¼ cup minced red onion

Sea salt or liquid aminos to taste

1 chopped ripe tomato

OPTIONAL ADDITIONS:

Minced bell peppers, hot peppers, or cayenne

Chopped cilantro or parsley

Raw pine nuts or sunflower seeds

Sun-dried tomatoes, soaked 15 minutes and chopped

Chopped black olives

Basil, oregano and rosemary for an Italian flavor

GINGER PUMPKIN SEED GUACAMOLE:

Use ¼ cup orange juice instead of lemon or lime juice

Add 1 cup raw pumpkin seeds or pepitas, soaked 10 minutes

Add ½ Tbsp fresh grated ginger, or 1 tsp ground ginger

Mash the avocado, then mix in citrus juice and spices. Fold in remaining ingredients, adding tomatoes last.

Serve Guacamole with dippin' veggies and Flax Crackers (page 78), or atop Carrot Chip Nachos (page 66). Serve it burrito-style in a cabbage or romaine lettuce leaf, with some salsa added. It's also a great accompaniment for Rawsome Rellenos (page 80).

Guacamole doesn't keep well, so if you make it ahead of time, squeeze citrus juice over the top, and leave the avocado pits in until right before serving time.

⊘ FRESH TOMATO SALSA

Use the best-quality, ripest tomatoes you can find.

1 ½ cups finely chopped ripe tomatoes

1-2 Tbsp fresh lemon or lime juice

Minced peppers of your choice, to taste

2 cloves garlic, minced

1 tsp sea salt, or to taste

½ cup chopped cilantro (optional)

SALSA VERDE:

Use green tomatoes, and include chopped parsley and basil

Toss all ingredients. If using hot peppers, add conservatively and let the salsa marinate for an hour before adding more.

Serve with sliced zucchini or Flax Crackers (page 78), or include in a pile of Carrot Chip Nachos (next page).

⊘ MANGO SALSA

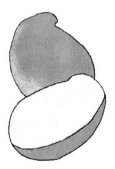

Is it dinner or dessert?

2 mangoes, chopped

1 small red onion, chopped

½ cup chopped cilantro

¼ cup fresh lime or lemon juice

Minced peppers of your choice, to taste

1 tsp sea salt, or to taste

Toss all ingredients. If using hot peppers, add conservatively and let the salsa marinate for an hour before adding more.

Serve with cucumber slices or Flax Crackers (page 78), or include in a pile of Carrot Chip Nachos (next page).

Ⓑ CREAMY TOMATILLO SALSA

If you enjoy this as much as I do, you'll make it a staple.

4 tomatillos, chopped

1 minced jalapeno, or peppers of your choice

½-1 Tbsp fresh lime juice

¼ cup fresh orange juice

½ tsp sea salt, or to taste

1 ripe avocado

Blend all ingredients until desired consistency. If using hot peppers, add conservatively and let the salsa marinate for an hour before adding more.

Serve with Flax Crackers (page 78), or include in a pile of Carrot Chip Nachos (see below), or alongside Rawsome Rellenos (page 80).

Ⓞ Ⓑ Ⓕ CARROT CHIP NACHOS

Assemble the layers to your taste, and it's a fiesta!

Thick carrot ends, cut into round "chips"

Kitchen Sink Guacamole (page 64)

Fresh Tomato (previous page) or Creamy Tomatillo Salsa (see above)

Refried Almonds (page 69), or Mexican Pate (page 70)

Chopped ripe tomatoes, lettuce and cilantro

Minced jalapeno, or hot peppers of your choice

Sweet carrots go very well with guacamole, dips, and salsas, so make this dish as simple or decadent as you wish. For a family or a party, make everything, including Flax Crackers (page 78), and call it a smorgasbord!

⊘ Ⓑ INSTANT CINNAMON FRUIT DIP

Simply heavenly.

½ cup raw cashew or macadamia butter, or sesame tahini

½ cup fresh orange juice or water

¼ cup pure honey or agave syrup OR ½ cup soft dates

1 tsp vanilla extract

1 Tbsp cinnamon or pumpkin pie spice

½ tsp orange zest

Blend or whisk nut butter with orange juice or water until smooth and creamy. Add the honey or agave syrup, or the dates two at a time, and then add the rest of the ingredients. Add more juice or water, until the dip reaches desired consistency.

If using a whisk, make sure your nut butter is at room temperature, and use honey or agave syrup.

Serve with sliced fruit. This dip is particularly good with tropical fruits, like banana and mango.

Ⓑ VERY BERRY FRUIT DIP

You won't believe what's in it.

1 ripe banana

½ ripe avocado (yup, avocado)

1 ½ cups mixed berries, fresh or frozen

1-2 Tbsp fresh lemon or orange juice

1-2 tsp lemon or orange zest

1 Tbsp pure honey or maple syrup, or ½ Tbsp date sugar

Chopped fresh mint, or a pinch of dried mint

Pinch of sea salt

Blend all ingredients until smooth and creamy.

Ⓑ CARAMEL FRUIT DIP

It's a carnival for your mouth. Happy fall!

2 cups dates (about 18 large), pitted

1/3 cup pure honey or agave syrup

½ tsp cinnamon

Soak the dates in water for about 30 minutes and then drain. (Save the soak water - it's great in smoothies!) Puree the dates with the honey until smooth, and then add cinnamon. If using a VitaMix, use 1/3 cup honey; you can use more if using a regular kitchen blender.

Serve with sliced multi-colored apples. If preparing ahead of time, coat slices with a little lemon juice to prevent browning.

⊘ Ⓕ NORI ROLLS

Fresh and tasty, and easier than you think.

Raw, untoasted nori sheets

EZ Nori Filling (next page), OR

Sweet & Sour Carrot Pate (page 70)

Thin strips of carrot, cucumber and bell pepper

Slices of avocado

Sprouts of your choice

Shredded cabbage or lettuce (optional)

Chopped cilantro (optional)

Cut a large sheet of nori in half. Spread about 3 Tbsp of your filling of choice along one of the narrow ends, ½ inch from the edge. Lay all your veggies on top of the filling, and roll the nori away from you, sealing the edge with a little water at the other end.

Serve with Nama Shoyu and wasabi. *Itadakimasu!*

 EZ NORI FILLING

Machine-free for quick preparation.

1/3 cup raw sesame tahini or almond butter, at room temperature

3 Tbsp unpasteurized miso

1 Tbsp pure honey or agave syrup

1 clove garlic, minced, or 1/8 tsp. garlic powder

½ tsp powdered ginger

¼ cup scallions, minced

1 Tbsp Nama Shoyu or wheat-free tamari, or more to taste

Mix all ingredients. Use in Nori Hand Rolls (previous page), or for dippin' veggies.

Ⓕ REFRIED ALMONDS

So rich and nutty, it almost tastes cooked.

1 cup raw almonds, soaked 8-12 hours

½ cup fresh lemon juice

1-2 cloves garlic, minced, or ¼ tsp garlic powder

¼ cup sun-dried tomatoes, soaked 15 minutes, chopped

¼ cup red onion

1 tsp each cumin, coriander and paprika

Pinch of cayenne

Sea salt to taste

Put all ingredients into a food processor with an S-blade. Process until smooth, or until the consistency of a traditional bean dip. Add a little water if needed.

Serve with dippin' veggies or Flax Crackers (page 78), or include in a pile of Carrot Chip Nachos (page 66).

(F) (B) VERSATILE SUNFLOWER PATE

A smooth, protein-packed basic pate.

2 cups sunflower seeds, sprouted (see page 40)

2 Tbsp raw sesame tahini

½ cup fresh lemon juice

1-2 Tbsp Nama Shoyu, wheat-free tamari or liquid aminos

1 large clove garlic, minced, or ¼ tsp garlic powder

¼ cup chopped scallions

Pinch of cayenne

You can sprout your own sunflower seeds, or buy them from a health food store. If you're short on time, you can simply soak the seeds for 30 minutes before using.

Put all ingredients into a food processor with an S-blade and process until smooth, occasionally scraping the sides of the food processor with a spatula to ensure uniform blending. A blender can be used instead if you add water to thin the pate.

Use as a dip for veggies or Flax Crackers (page 78); to stuff celery sticks, avocadoes, tomatoes, or bell peppers; or as a base for one of the variations below.

Asian Pate: Mix in by hand 1 cup (total) of chopped veggies of your choice, including red onions, bell pepper, celery, bok choy, parsley, and/or cilantro. Mix in a little Citrus Ginger Marinade to bind the ingredients.

Mexican Pate: Substitute lime juice for lemon juice. Mix in by hand ½ cup each minced carrots, celery, zucchini, red onion, and chopped cilantro. Add 2 tsp marjoram or thyme, and cayenne or minced hot peppers to taste. Use as a dip, or to stuff Rawsome Rellenos (page 80).

Sweet & Sour Carrot Pate: Mix in by hand 2-3 Tbsp minced red onion, and 1 cup of carrot pulp, which you can procure from your nearest fresh juice bar. Add 1-2 Tbsp fresh grated ginger and additional lemon juice and cayenne to taste. Use as a dip, or as a filling for Nori Rolls (previous page).

CHAPTER 7:
DEHYDRATION FOR THE ROAD

Machine-free dehydration is possible, but only if you live in a *very* hot climate and can dry your food in the sun! As for the rest of us...

If I were to recommend any machine for busy people, besides a blender, it would be a dehydrator.

Dried foods are extremely convenient for people on the go, since they'll keep well in a desk drawer, glove compartment or backpack.

Using a dehydrator is easy and foolproof. Simply set the temperature to about 108°F, put the food in, and turn the machine on. The recommended drying times are extremely flexible; I've forgotten about my dehydrating food for up to an extra twelve hours, and all was well.

By dehydrating your own foods, you'll be able to avoid commercially dried foods and fruit, which are cooked at high temperatures and often include added oil, sweeteners, chemicals and preservatives.

You can buy a simple dehydrator for only around $40-80 from Nesco. See the Resources section for mail-order sources, or check your local appliance stores. Order some extra solid drying sheets too, which will be necessary for drying fruit leather, flax crackers and cookies.

See Appendix II for further details about dehydrators, and for instructions on how to dry fresh herbs.

Raw Foods for Busy People

DRIED FRUIT

It doesn't get any simpler than this.

Fruit of your choice, sliced

Use literally any fruit you'd like. Bananas and apples are easy. Strawberries, mango and kiwis are especially tasty.

Fill your dehydrator trays with thinly sliced fruit of your choice. Turn your dehydrator on, and allow fruit to dry for 8-12 hours or more at 108°. To be dry enough for storage, the fruit should be leathery in texture, and no beads of moisture should form when the fruit is torn.

Use solid dehydrator sheets when drying small fruit, like blueberries. Otherwise, use the slotted trays.

Dry your own fruit to use in Live Trail Mix (page 87).

B D FRUIT LEATHER

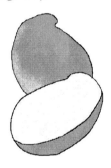

Let your imagination run wild!

2 cups of fruit

1 cup of juice or water

Put fruit of your choice into a blender with 1 cup of liquid, such as water, apple juice, grape juice, orange juice, or coconut water. Add a dash of sea salt. Liquefy until smooth, pour out onto solid dehydrator sheets, and dehydrate until dry, about 12-20 hours at 108°.

Apple or Pear Cinnamon Leather: 2 peeled and cored apples or pears, with 1 cup of apple juice or water, and 1 tsp of cinnamon.

Mixed Berry Leather: Blend 2 cups of fresh or frozen berries with 1 cup of apple juice, grape juice, or water.

Tropical Fruit Leather: Blend 2 cups of mango, pineapple, banana, and/or kiwis with 1 cup of orange juice or water. Fresh young coconut meat, and young coconut water can be added as well.

⚙ SWEET SEED BARS

Sticky sweet and perfectly portable.

2 cups sesame/hemp/sunflower/pumpkin seed mix

5-6 Tbsp pure honey, or agave or maple syrup

Pinch of sea salt

VARIATION 1: Add 1-2 Tbsp lemon or orange juice

VARIATION 2: Add ½ Tbsp Vanilla extract and ½ tsp cinnamon

Soak sunflower and pumpkin seeds for 10 minutes before using, or sprout sunflower seeds by soaking in water for 8-12 hours. Mix all ingredients together with your hands. Shape into thin bars on solid dehydrator sheets. Dehydrate at 108° for 8-12 hours, or until dry enough to remove from the solid sheets. Move bars to slotted dehydrator trays, and dehydrate for another 4-8 hours, or until dry on all sides.

When mixing the batch, wet your hands to prevent too much sticking. A wet, stiff rubber spatula may be used to shape the bars on the dehydrator sheets.

⚙ CITRUS ZESTS

Keep these around and sprinkle them on everything.

Fresh grated rind of lemon, lime or orange

Any time you're going to be juicing a few lemons, limes or oranges, consider making zest from the rind.

Finely grate the outer rind of your citrus fruit, before juicing it, and place the shavings on a solid dehydrator sheet. Dehydrate at 108° for about an hour, or until dry. For a fine consistency, you can grind the dried zest in a seed or coffee grinder. Either way, it's great to have around when you need it, and it makes an attractive garnish too.

Ⓓ NUT BUTTER COOKIES

To make this recipe without a food processor, buy your nuts already ground, or just use dried coconut. Otherwise, you can use a food processor to grind the nuts.

3 cups total ground nuts and/or dried coconut

½ cup raw almond or cashew butter, at room temperature

¾ cup pure maple syrup or honey

2 Tbsp cold-pressed olive or flaxseed oil

1 Tbsp vanilla extract

Pinch of sea salt

CAROB COOKIES: Add ¼ cup raw carob powder

SPICE COOKIES: Add 1 Tbsp cinnamon and ½ Tbsp nutmeg

BANANA COOKIES: Replace 1 cup nuts with dried banana

Mix all ingredients by hand or with a food processor. Shape into cookies (see below), and place on solid dehydrator sheets. Dehydrate for 8-12 hours at 108°, and then move cookies to slotted dehydrator trays. Dehydrate for another 4-8 hours or more, until dry on the outside.

If you're as lazy (er... I mean busy) as I am, you'll like this trick I use for shaping cookies. If your cookie dough turns out too stiff or dry, shaping the cookies will require either rolling and re-rolling the dough out between wax paper sheets and cutting it, or shaping it into unattractive wads with your hands. My shortcut includes adding water to the cookie dough until it's soft enough to be formed into pliable balls. I then place a solid dehydrator sheet in front of me on the counter and throw each ball of dough at the sheet. They "splat" into perfect cookie shapes, with no trouble at all! Adding water makes for extra drying time, of course, but I don't mind waiting. *That's* effortless.

ⓓ CRISPY ONION TOPPERS

These are great on salads, or to top off any vegetable dish. Use on top of the Barbecue Portobello on page 49.

Two large onions

1 cup Nama Shoyu or wheat-free tamari

1/3 cup cold-pressed olive oil

Garlic powder, cayenne or Chinese 5-spice (optional)

Slice onion into ringlets and marinate in tamari, olive oil and spices, for 1 to 8 hours. Remove ringlets from marinade and dry on solid dehydrator sheets at 108° for 12-20 hours, or until crisp.

ⓓ VEGETABLE KABOBS

Serve with a salad, the Barbecue Portobello, or Nori Rolls.

Zucchini or yellow squash

Mushrooms of any kind

Peppers and Onions

Cherry tomatoes

Cauliflower and Broccoli

Carrot slices

Cut vegetables into large chunks and rounds. Use any marinade of your choice from Chapter 4.

Marinate the vegetables for at least 2 hours at room temperature, or overnight in the refrigerator. Skewer your veggies, and dehydrate at 108° for up to 24 hours, or until as soft as desired. To reheat, return cold Kabobs to the dehydrator for one hour.

Ⓓ FLAVORED NUTS & SEEDS

A great alternative to popcorn, and easier to sneak into the theatre.

2-4 cups nuts and seeds of your choice

SALTY NUT MARINADE:

Nama Shoyu, wheat-free tamari, or sea salt dissolved in water

Crushed garlic, or garlic powder (optional)

Crushed red pepper or cayenne (optional)

HONEY NUT MARINADE:

(for 2 cups of nuts and seeds)

¼ cup pure honey, agave or maple syrup

1 ½ Tbsp vanilla extract

Pinch of sea salt

Cinnamon and nutmeg (optional)

Chili powder (optional)

Cover nuts and seeds with the Salty Marinade, or toss with the Sweet Marinade. Marinate for 30 minutes to 12 hours (the longer the stronger). Spread on mesh or solid dehydrator sheets, depending on the size of the seed or nut, and dehydrate at 108° for 12-24 hours, or until dry.

If using the Sweet Marinade, soak the nuts or seeds in water for at least 10-30 minutes before tossing. Ideally, nuts and seeds should be thoroughly soaked, so if you have the time, soak almonds and sunflower seeds for 8-12 hours; walnuts and pumpkin seeds for 2-4 hours; cashews for 30 minutes; and all other nuts 4-6 hours.

Serve as a snack, or toss with a green salad, coleslaw, or Pineapple Waldorf Salad (page 37).

⚙ FLAX CRACKERS

Try this experiment: Soak ½ cup of flax seeds in ¼ cup of water for 30-60 minutes. Stick your finger in it. Now you know why flax crackers are so easy to make: It's the goo!

2 cups flax seeds

1 ½ cups water

Salt, spices or vegetables (see below)

½ cup sesame or hemp seeds (optional)

For a blender-free version, soak flax seeds as described above, spread the flax seed goo onto solid dehydrator sheets, and sprinkle with your choice of salt, garlic powder, Italian seasonings, cayenne, or Chinese 5-spice.

For more complex flavors, you can use a blender to liquefy the veggies and spices of your choice in the water, before adding to the flax seeds for soaking (see below). If using wet vegetables, like tomatoes, reduce the water to 1 cup.

Dehydrate for 2-4 hours at 108°, and then move crackers to slotted trays and dehydrate for 4-8 hours more, or until crisp.

A stiff spatula works well to spread the flax goo onto the dehydrator sheets. If you don't have enough solid dehydrator sheets for all the goo you've got, you can spread the goo onto pieces of waxed paper. If you use waxed paper, however, you must watch your drying time carefully and remove the crackers from the paper after about 3-4 hours. If the crackers are left on waxed paper for too long, they'll be stubbornly stuck together.

Sample Variations:
Mexican Flax Crackers: Blend water with fresh tomatoes, cilantro, lime juice, peppers, garlic, and sea salt.
Italian Flax Crackers: Blend water with tomatoes, zucchini, garlic, Italian seasoning, fresh basil, olives, bell peppers, and sea salt.
Asian Flax Crackers: Blend water with Nama Shoyu, lemon juice, cilantro, peppers, garlic, and Chinese 5-spice.

Ⓕ Ⓓ PESTO-STUFFED VEGETABLES

These make great hors d'oeuvres.
Oh, and a good pesto deserves fresh garlic.

1/3 cup pine nuts, soaked 10-20 minutes

2-3 cloves fresh garlic, minced

½ cup chopped parsley

½ cup chopped fresh basil

1 Tbsp cold-pressed olive oil

Pinch of sea salt

SPINACH PESTO: Substitute ½ cup of chopped spinach for ¼ cup of

the parsley

PESTO ALFREDO SAUCE: See Appendix I

Mushroom caps

Bell pepper chunks

Zucchini or yellow squash rounds

Grind the pine nuts in a food processor, or pound them in a mortar. Add the garlic and olive oil to the nuts, and process or pound until blended. Gradually add the greens and pulse chop or pound until finely chopped. Salt to taste. Put a dollop of pesto onto each vegetable piece, and dehydrate for 3-4 Hours at 108°.

Regularly scrape the sides of the food processor with a spatula to ensure uniform blending and consistency. You can make the pesto ahead and allow it to marinate overnight.

If another item is dehydrating at the same time, put the pesto veggies on the bottom. Pesto drippings don't taste very well on cookies!

If serving as hors d'oeuvres, drizzle each piece with olive oil, garnish with whole pine nuts, and serve with whole raw olives.

ⓕ ⓓ RAWSOME RELLENOS

Muy bien!

One batch of Mexican Pate (page 70)

Anaheim peppers, or peppers of your choice

Zucchini "boats"

Slice your peppers down the middle lengthwise, or bell peppers into three or four strips, along the indentations. Remove the seeds. For zucchini, cut in half lengthwise and remove the seeds with a spoon. Fill each pepper or zucchini boat with Mexican Pate, and dehydrate for 6-8 hours at 108°.

If you're not sure what kind of pepper to use, choose Anaheims. You can use hotter ones if you're so inclined, or just use bell peppers or zucchini if you're a spice wimp. If you're serving guests, use a variety of peppers of various colors. These are great served with cold Creamy Tomatillo Salsa, made on the mild side (page 66), or with Sour Cream (page 48).

ⓓ BUCKWHEAT GRANOLA

A delicious, crunchy, gluten-free cereal or snack.

2 cups raw buckwheat groats, sprouted

1 cup raw almonds or pecans, sliced or chopped

1 cup raisins or chopped dates, or a mix

½ Tbsp cinnamon

Pure agave syrup or honey to coat

HEMP SEED MILK: Blend ½ cup hemp seeds with 1 quart water, about

2 inches of vanilla bean (optional), and agave syrup or honey to taste

To sprout buckwheat, soak in water for 5-6 hours and then keep in a strainer for 24 hours at room temperature, rinsing a few times. Combine all ingredients and dehydrate on solid sheets for about 36 hours.

Serve with Hemp Seed Milk or Instant Almond Milk (p. 89).

CHAPTER 8:
DESSERTS, SNACKS & SHAKES

You could eat any of the following desserts for breakfast, lunch and dinner, and still be eating better than you ever have in your life.

Desserts are our friends. Our sweet tooth is natural: it is our innate propensity toward fresh fruit. After all, if you're in a natural setting, and you have a sweet tooth, what do you reach for? Fruit, of course!

Unfortunately, our natural taste for sweet fruit is working against us in the modern world, since our taste buds have been exposed to artificial and concentrated sugars not found in nature.

But never fear. This chapter will have you on a healthy course in no time. How about some vitamins, enzymes, fiber and pure water to go with your (natural) sugar? What a concept!

FRUIT COMBINING DIAGRAM

Guidelines for fruit combining can be helpful, not only for optimal digestion, but for flavor combining when putting together different types of fruit for smoothies and fruit platters.

The general rules are as follows:
1. Sweet fruits combine best with sub-acid fruits.
2. Melons should be eaten alone, but can be combined with acid or sub-acid fruits.
3. Generally, any non-sweet fruit (cucumber, tomato, avocado), as well as celery and leafy greens, will combine well with fruits.

Grapes
Bananas
Papaya
SWEET FRUIT
Dried Fruit
Dates
Figs

Apples
Apricots, Pears
Mango, Papaya
SUB-ACID FRUIT
Cherries, Kiwi
Blueberries
Peaches

Cantaloupe
Watermelon
Honey Dew
MELONS
Musk Melon
Crenshaw
Casaba

Pineapple
Sour Apples
Raspberries
ACID FRUIT
Blackberries
Strawberries
Citrus

⊘ CINNAMON STEWED FRUIT

Forget the cooked, lifeless version.
This marinated fruit is full of natural flavor.

4 ripe apples, pears, or peaches, sliced

2 Tbsp fresh lemon juice

1 tsp lemon zest

½ cup apple juice

1 Tbsp cinnamon or pumpkin pie spice

1 Tbsp pure agave or maple syrup (optional)

½ cup raisins or currants (optional)

¼ cup chopped or ground pecans or nuts (optional)

Toss all ingredients and allow to marinate for at least an hour, allowing the lemon juice to soften the fruit.

Top with Whipped Cashew Cream (page 96) for an additional dimension of flavor.

⊘ BERRIES ROMANOFF

Traditionally made with a dash of Cointreau liqueur.

1 pint fresh strawberries or mixed berries

½ cup fresh orange juice

½ tsp orange zest

2 Tbsp date sugar or agave syrup

½ tsp cinnamon (optional)

Chopped almonds to garnish

Simply marinate the strawberries for an hour or more, and enjoy.

Top this dessert off with Orange Cashew Cream (page 96) for a truly decadent treat.

⊘ SWEET FRUIT SALAD

A treat for breakfast or dessert.

1/2 cup pure maple syrup or agave syrup

3 Tbsp fresh orange or pineapple juice

½ tsp orange, lemon or lime zest

4 to 6 cups diced fresh fruit

Romaine lettuce or spinach leaves

Mix syrup, juice and zest together, and gently toss with fruit. Marinate for at least 30 minutes, stirring a few times.
Serve on large whole romaine or spinach leaves.

⊘ SPICED FRUIT SALAD

This is great for a party!

½ cup pure agave syrup or honey

½ cup fresh grapefruit juice

Juice of 1 lime

¼ tsp nutmeg or pumpkin pie spice

Pinch of sea salt

3 cups chopped fruit, including grapefruit pulp and strawberries

1 large avocado, diced

Toss all ingredients with lettuce and serve.

⊘ PINEAPPLE CARROTS

Consider this a machine-free carrot cake!

2-3 cups grated carrots

½ cup each chopped pineapple and raisins

1 Tbsp fresh lemon juice

½ cup pineapple or orange juice

1 tsp each cinnamon, nutmeg and powdered ginger

Dash of vanilla extract

4-6 pineapple rings

¼ cup chopped walnuts

¼ cup parsley, to garnish

Toss all ingredients except the pineapple rings and garnishes, and marinate for at least an hour, allowing the juices to soften the carrots.

Serve the marinated carrots on top of each pineapple ring, and garnish. Add Lemon Whipped Cream (page 96) if desired.

⊘ SWEET SPREADS

Lick it off your hands, and feel like a kid again.

Raw almond or cashew butter, OR

¼ cup tahini mashed with 1 Tbsp honey or agave syrup

Celery or carrot sticks

Apple slices, with fresh berries

Banana, with Carob Sauce (page 89)

A batch of Nut Butter Cookies (page 75)

Smear nut butter and sweetened tahini on absolutely anything.

⊘ Ⓓ LIVE TRAIL MIX

It's energy for the road.

Goji berries

Raisins - golden, red and black

Dried cranberries

Dried banana slices

Dried figs, apricots, mangoes and pineapple, chopped

Dried shaved coconut pieces

Sunflower and pumpkin seeds

Fresh nuts - almonds, walnuts, pecans, cashews, etc.

Flavored nuts and seeds (see previous chapter)

Raw cacao nibs

Buckwheat Granola pieces (page 80)

Assemble or create your live trail mix ingredients, and mix together.
   See the previous chapter for instructions on dehydrating fruit and flavored nuts.

⊘ DATE POPPERS

Do the sticky part at home, and they trael well.

Fresh large, dry dates, such as Medjool

Whole Brazil nuts, cashews or almonds, or halved walnuts or pecans

Cut each date in half and remove the pit and cap. Stuff each date with a nut, and go!

⊘ NIRVANA BARS

Roll up your sleeves for this one!

4 cups ground raw walnuts

1 cup ground raw cashews, macadamias or almonds

1 cup raw sunflower and/or pumpkin seeds

1 cup dried coconut (optional)

½ cup raw carob powder (optional)

1 cup raw almond butter (at room temperature)

½ cup pure maple syrup, or more to taste

¼ cup cold-pressed flaxseed oil

Pinch of sea salt

Toss the nuts, seeds, coconut and carob powder together first. Whip the almond butter, maple syrup, oil and salt together separately, either with a whisk or in a food processor. Using your hands, mash all the ingredients together until the nut mixture is completely coated.

The mixture should be fairly dry while you're working with it, so spend some time really mashing it all together. If the mixture is too wet, it won't stand up in solid bars after refrigerating.

Refrigerate in a short, rectangular container for at least 3 hours, and then cut into bars. It's raw candy!

Ⓑ INSTANT CREAMER

Enjoy in your favorite tea, or over fruit or raw granola.

1 Tbsp raw cashew butter OR ¼ cup cashews, soaked 30 min.

½ - ¾ cup water

INSTANT ALMOND MILK:

1 Tbsp raw almond butter

½ cup water

Blend until smooth and creamy.
    This makes a healthy creamer for any beverage. You can also pour it over fresh strawberries, bananas or peaches, or purchase raw granola from one of the companies listed in the Resources section.

 CAROB SAUCE

This goes well on just about anything.

1 cup raw carob powder

½ cup pitted soft dates, soaked 10 minutes

½ cup pure maple or agave syrup

2 Tbsp cold-pressed olive or coconut oil (optional)

2 Tbsp vanilla extract (optional)

MEXICAN CAROB SAUCE: Add 2 tsp cinnamon

A blender works best with this sauce, though you can use a whisk if you substitute additional syrup for the dates, and use the olive or coconut oil and some elbow grease. Add a little water to thin, if desired.

⊘ Ⓑ CREAMY PUDDINGS

Avocado, banana and soft nuts make creamy puddings.

AVOCADO BASED PUDDING:

1 ripe avocado

1 ripe banana OR ¼ cup pitted dates, soaked 10 minutes

½ cup berries OR ¼ cup raw carob powder

2 tsp vanilla extract

BANANA BASED PUDDING:

1 ripe banana

6 dates, soaked up to 30 minutes

2-3 peaches, or meat and water from one young coconut

2 tsp vanilla extract

1 tsp cinnamon (optional)

NUT BASED PUDDING:

1 cup cashews soaked 30 minutes, or almonds soaked 8 hours

½ cup water, fresh orange juice or coconut water

1 ripe banana OR ¼ cup pitted dates, soaked 10 minutes

½ cup dried or fresh coconut (optional)

Sliced banana or fresh berries of your choice

For the avocado and banana based puddings, simply whip up all ingredients in a blender, or mash and whisk by hand if not using dates. Use a spatula to scrape the sides of the blender a few times during blending.

For the nut-based puddings, blend the nuts and water or juice first, until truly smooth, before adding the rest of the ingredients.

Top with Whipped Cashew Cream (page 96) if desired.

 ICE DREAM

A natural, frozen treat.

2 cups frozen fruit of your choice

2 Tbsp sweetener of your choice

¼ cup raw carob powder (optional)

¼ cup fruit juice OR Instant Creamer or Almond Milk (optional) (page 89)

Softer fruits work best, such as bananas, strawberries, peaches and mangoes.

Peel your fruit, if desired, before cutting it into small pieces and freezing.

Add sweetener, carob powder and/or nut milk to the frozen fruit and mash either with a potato masher or in a food processor. Enjoy right away or re-freeze.

To make a sundae, top with Carob Sauce (page 89), Whipped Cashew Cream (page 96) and chopped nuts.

Ⓑ HALVAH SHAKE

Sesame tahini makes for a rich and creamy shake.

2-3 Tbsp raw sesame tahini

1 Tbsp raw almond butter

1 fresh or frozen ripe banana

2 dates, or 1 Tbsp pure honey or agave syrup

Dash of vanilla extract

3-4 Tbsp raw carob powder (optional)

½-1 cup water

Blend all ingredients until smooth and creamy. Add a few ice cubes if desired. *Tip:* Peel bananas before freezing.

Ⓑ PRE-WORKOUT SHAKE #1

What you want for energy: simple sugars and EFAs.

1 cup fresh orange or apple juice

1 Tbsp cold-pressed coconut, flax or an EFA blend oil

1 banana

½ cup mango, fresh or frozen

2 pitted dates

Handful of mixed berries (optional)

1-2 tsp spirulina or other green powder (optional)

Blend all ingredients until smooth.

Ⓑ PRE-WORKOUT SHAKE #2

The energy of cacao comes from theobromine - "food of the gods."

1 cup apple juice or water

1 Tbsp cold-pressed coconut, flax or an EFA blend oil

½ cup mixed berries, fresh or frozen

2 pitted dates

3 Tbsp raw cacao nibs

1-2 tsp maca powder

1-2 tsp spirulina or other green powder (optional)

Blend all ingredients until smooth.

Ⓑ CARAMEL APPLE SHAKE

Decadence in a glass.

1 apple, cut in chunks

1 cup apple juice

2-3 Tbsp raw almond butter

2 Tbsp pure maple syrup, OR 3 pitted soft dates

Dash of cinnamon and nutmeg

1 ripe banana (optional)

ORANGE PECAN SHAKE:

Use ½ cup pecans instead of almond butter

Add ¼ cup raisins soaked in ¼ cup orange juice

Add a dash of orange zest

Blend all ingredients until smooth.

Ⓑ JORDAN'S POWER SHAKE

When you want something heavier, or for after a workout.

Meat and water from one young coconut

1-2 Tbsp protein or supplement powder of your choice

¼ - ½ cup fresh orange juice

2 Tbsp raw almond butter (optional)

Dash of vanilla extract (optional)

Blend all ingredients until smooth.

⊕ DATE NUT LOGS

Now, you'll know how to make your own.

1 cup pitted dates, soaked up to 30 minutes

½ cup dates, dried apricots or figs, soaked 30 minutes

1 cup raw pecans, walnuts or almonds, ground

1 cup dried coconut

1 tsp cinnamon or pumpkin pie spice

Grind dry nuts in a food processor, or buy your nuts ground. Add coconut first, and then cinnamon and vanilla. Finally, add dates and other dried fruit a few pieces at a time. Shape batter into small logs ½-3/4 inch thick, and roll in dried coconut. Chill until stiff.

⊕ PARTY BALLS

Eat these ungarnished, or dress them up for a party.

1 cup raw almonds, ground

2 Tbsp pine nuts or cashews or macadamias, ground

½ cup dried shredded coconut

¼ cup raw almond butter

¼ cup pure honey or syrup, or more to hold balls together

CAROB BALLS: Add 1 cup raw carob powder + ¼ cup water

Combine the nuts, coconut, and carob powder, if using, in a food processor with an S-blade. Mix the almond butter, sweetener, and water if needed, separately, and then add to the dry ingredients. The dough should be fairly dry, but wet enough to hold together when rolled into balls. If you're dressing them up, roll each ball in carob powder, or finely ground coconut or almonds. Refrigerate several hours, until firm.

ⓑ VANILLA-CACAO LATTE

Use raw cacao for a new-fashioned cappuccino! Use a nut-milk bag for extra smoothness.

½ cup raw cacao beans, soaked overnight in 2 cups water

2 Tbsp raw cashew, macadamia or almond butter

2 Tbsp raw sesame tahini or hemp seed butter

2-3 Tbsp pure agave syrup or honey

1 tsp pure vanilla extract

Pinch of sea salt

2 Tbsp powdered maca (optional)

FLAVORED LATTE: Replace 1 cup water with strong tea, such as mint, orange or raspberry

RICH CHOCOLATE MILK: Use ½ cup raw carob powder, or more to taste, in place of cacao beans

If, like many busy people, you have a taste for specialty coffee drinks, you'll enjoy this rich, healthy alternative.

Combine soaked cacao beans and water with the nut and seed butters, and blend for several minutes. Put this mixture through a nut-milk bag or a fine strainer to remove the solid pieces. Take your time with the nut-milk bag, if using, squeezing gently so as not to tear it. Return the liquid to the blender, adding the rest of the ingredients, including sweetener, vanilla, salt, and maca, if using. Blend well. The heat of a Vita-Mix will warm the beverage, or you can warm it using a double boiler.

Interestingly, raw cacao does not cause the excitement of the nervous and circulatory systems, or the accelerated pulse, often caused by roasted cacao. Enjoy your cacao latte in good health!

To make Rich Chocolate Milk, no soaking is required. Simply blend all ingredients. Using a nut-milk bag is still recommended for a super-smooth beverage.

Ⓑ WHIPPED CASHEW CREAM

One taste of this and you'll never go back to dairy.

1 ½ cups raw cashews, soaked 30 minutes

½ cup water, or juice to flavor (see below)

4-5 dates, soaked 30 minutes

1 tsp vanilla or almond extract

ORANGE CREAM: Use fresh orange juice + a dash of orange zest

APPLE CREAM: Use apple juice + a dash of cinnamon

LEMON CREAM: Use 1/3 cup lemon juice + ¼ cup honey or syrup

COCONUT CREAM: Use coconut water + extra vanilla

In a blender, combine the nuts and water or juice first. Blend until smooth and creamy. Add the dates two at a time, and then the remaining ingredients. Use a spatula to scrape the sides of the blender a few times during blending. Be patient, and make sure it gets real smooth.

This is a healthy topping for any dessert, or to complement fresh berries or sliced bananas.

APPENDIX I:
LIVE VEGGIE PASTA

Making live pasta out of zucchini and squash is a great alternative—it's wheat-free, high fiber, enzyme rich and made from healthy carbs. There are a few easy ways to cut your veggie pasta, and marinating it will help create the familiar texture of cooked grain pastas. Raw marinara and pesto sauces are heavenly – see the following page for recipes.

Cutting the Pasta—A Saladacco or Spirooli spiralizer will quickly create spaghetti or fettuccine-style noodles. Some electric juicers come with an attachment for cutting veggie pastas. You can also cut zucchini pasta into strips, by hand or with a mandoline.

Spirooli spiralizer   *Saladacco spiralizer*

Marinating—You can use olive oil and a bit of sea salt to soften your raw pasta into a more familiar texture and consistency. Use 1/4 cup olive oil for two medium zucchini. Toss a few times within about 15 minutes.

Warming Raw Foods—You can safely warm your sauces in a double boiler just until warm to the touch, and pastas in a dehydrator or warm oven for about 30 minutes.

 SIMPLE PORTOBELLO PASTA

2 Portobello mushroom caps, sliced

1 clove garlic, crushed, or 1/8 tsp garlic powder

3 Tb cold-pressed olive oil

2 Tb Nama Shoyu, wheat-free tamari or liquid aminos

2 Tb Italian Seasoning

Marinate all ingredients for about one hour and then toss with pasta and chopped ripe tomatoes.

 SPINACH PESTO SAUCE

1/3 cup pine nuts, soaked 10-20 minutes

2 cloves fresh garlic, minced

½ cup chopped spinach

½ cup chopped fresh basil

¼ cup chopped parsley

½ cup cold-pressed olive oil

Pinch of sea salt

Grind the pine nuts with garlic and olive oil first, in a food processor, then add the greens gradually and pulse blend. Otherwise, use a mortar and pestle to grind the nuts and garlic, then combine with oil and finely chopped greens.

PESTO ALFREDO SAUCE:

Reduce olive oil to 2 Tbsp then pulse blend pesto with:

1 cup raw cashews, soaked for 30 minutes in ¾ cup water

1 Tbsp fresh lemon juice

Pinch of thyme

Blend cashews, water, lemon juice and thyme until smooth, then add the pesto to blender and pulse blend.

APPENDIX II:
DEHYDRATORS

I always recommend dehydrators for busy people because you can make portable foods to stash in your desk, backpack, glove compartment, etc.

Temperature - To preserve enzymes, dry foods at about 108°.

Modern dehydrators - The Excalibur dehydrator (below left), is popular for its spaciousness, versatility and longevity. The removable trays help you adjust the "head room" for drying taller items like pie crusts and stuffed mushrooms, and the large tray area allows easy drying of full-size pie and pizza crusts, as well as large batches of flax crackers.

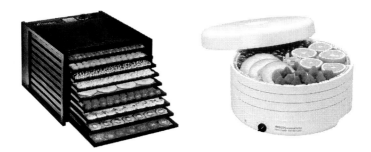

Economy dehydrators - Brands like the round Nesco dehydrator (above right) are relatively inexpensive and are best for fruit, herbs and other small items. Buy an extra tray and cut out the grid to create "head room," and make individual pie and pizza crusts that will fit on the narrow, circular trays.

Electric oven - Some people experiment using their oven when first starting out. This can work for foods that don't need much drying time, like pie crusts, flavored nuts, herbs and zests, and flax crackers. Set your oven to its lowest heat setting, and if necessary, prop the door open so it doesn't get too hot for too long. For your safety, do not prop open a gas oven door.

Hot sun - Drying foods in the sun is appropriate where temperatures reach 105°F or more. Quicker drying for fruit and large items may happen on a suspended net or mesh, rather than on a flat surface.

 DRIED HERBS

Dry your own herbs to preserve enzymes, flavor and freshness. Plus, your home will smell wonderful!

Herbs are dry enough when they're crisp and brittle. If condensation is created when the herbs are stored in an airtight container, they're not dry enough.

Drying leaves - Time: 1-3 hours at 90-100°F
When drying small leaves, you can either place a whole stalk or stem of the herb in the dehydrator, or lay a mesh sheet on top of the leaves so they won't blow around once dry. Store in a dry, dark place. Popular choices include chives, dill, marjoram, mint, oregano, parsley, rosemary, sage and thyme.

Drying basil leaves - Time: 18-24 hours at 90-100°F
Basil leaves can be quite full and thick, so they take longer to dry. Break the veins to reduce drying time. Store in a dry, dark place.

Drying seeds - Time: 2-5 hours at 90-100°F
Dry seeds by placing a whole stalk in your dehydrator after rinsing in hot water. Choices include anise, caraway, coriander, cumin, mustard, and fennel. You can also dry flax seeds and then grind them to make a fiber cleansing supplement.

Garlic cloves - Time: 6-12 hours at 90-100°F
Peel several heads of garlic cloves, and then halve or slice to dry. Reduce drying time by slicing very thin with a sharp knife.

Ginger root - Time: 2-5 hours at 90-100°F
Rinse or scrub the outside of the ginger root and then slice. Reduce drying time by slicing very thin with a sharp knife.

Chili peppers - Time: 5-12 hours at 90-100°F
Slice chili pepper pods and dry for grinding, or mince very fine to make flakes.

Citrus Zests - See page 74.

Grinding powders - Use a seed or coffee grinder to create your own powdered herbs. This works well with garlic, ginger, chili powder, mustard and cumin seeds, sage, and even a blend of Italian seasonings, like basil, oregano, marjoram, thyme and rosemary.

APPENDIX III:
SEASONAL PRODUCE

Eating produce that is in season and grown in your local region is the best way to guarantee that the food you eat is packed with maximum nutrition. Produce that is ripened on the tree or vine and is not stored for long periods of time will have higher levels of vitamins and minerals. In fact, it is fairly common for commercial fruit to be picked "green" (unripe) and then transported long distances or stored for up to two years. It may even be spray-painted before being shipped to the stores to be sold! Studies of oranges that have been treated this way show that the fruit has *no Vitamin C at all!*

When you purchase local, seasonal produce, you are further assured that your food is organic by U.S. standards. Any produce that is grown in other countries is *organic by that country's standards only*; it is not tested in the U.S. even if the American distributor is certified as an organic company.

The list below is a general one for the U.S. For information regarding your locality, check the internet or inquire at local farmers' markets and produce outlets.

YEAR-ROUND PRODUCE

Avocadoes	**Herbs**
Lemons	**Kale**
Oranges	**Leeks**
Beans	**Lettuce**
Beets	**Mushrooms**
Broccoli	**Onions**
Cabbage	**Potatoes**
Carrots	**Radishes**
Chard	**Spinach**
Endive	

SPRING

Fruits & Nuts	Vegetables
Berries	Arugula
Cherimoyas	Artichokes
Cherries	Asparagus
Grapefruit	Bok Choy
Limes	Cauliflower
Mandarins	Dandelion
Tangerines	Parsnips
Walnuts	Rutabaga
	Turnips

SUMMER

Fruits & Nuts	Vegetables
Apricots	Arugula
Blackberries	Basil
Blueberries	Celery
Cherries	Corn
Figs	Cucumbers
Grapes	Eggplant
Melons	Mustard
Nectarines	Okra
Peaches	Peas
Plums	Peppers
Raspberries	Shallots
Strawberries	Summer Squash
Tomatoes	

AUTUMN

Fruits & Nuts	Vegetables
Almonds	Artichokes
Apples	Arugula
Chestnuts	Bok Choy
Dates	Brussels Sprouts
Figs	Cauliflower
Grapefruit	Corn
Grapes	Cucumbers
Kiwi	Okra
Limes	Olives
Melons	Parsnips
Peaches	Peas
Pears	Peppers
Pistachios	Rutabaga
Plums	Winter Squash
Pomegranates	Sweet Potatoes
Raspberries	Tomatoes
Rhubarb	Turnips
Tomatoes	

WINTER

Fruits & Nuts	Vegetables
Cherimoyas	Bok Choy
Grapefruit	Brussels Sprouts
Kiwi	Cauliflower
Limes	Dandelion
Mandarins	Gourds
Pears	Parsnips
Persimmons	Rutabaga
Tangerines	Turnips
Walnuts	

APPENDIX IV:
TRANSITION STRATEGIES & BABY STEPS

Having a transition plan that suits your goals, personality and situation can ensure your success. Look over the suggestions below and consider which would be appropriate for your current situation. Which is more appropriate for making everyday changes? Which would be better when you're not so busy, when you have some time off from work or school? Which have you tried before, and what were your results?

A.M. to P.M.

Start eating raw foods first thing in the morning and then gradually eat only raw foods until a later hour in the day. This is a great way to slowly learn the skills and habits necessary to support a raw food diet. And, this allows you to stop at any step along the way, as it feels right to you.

1. Fresh fruit in a.m. and wait 30 minutes before eating anything else
2. Eat only fresh fruit and juices before noon
3. Eat only fresh fruit and juices in the morning and then a fresh salad with lunch
4. Eat only raw foods before 5pm, including a raw dressing (or cold-pressed olive oil and fresh lemon) on your lunch salad
5. Eat only raw foods and juices all day long and then a fresh salad with dinner
6a. Settle into step #5, removing processed grains, white sugar and non-organic dairy products from your diet
6b. Easily transition from step #5 to a 100% raw food or natural hygiene diet

Raw Before Cooked

When you eat cooked food on an empty stomach, your immune system will attack the food as it would attack a tumor in your body. This causes a spike in white blood cells, called "leukocytosis" which is a waste of your immune system's vital resources. To get your immune system rebalanced and refocused on invaders and tumors:

Make the commitment to eat an equal amount of raw food before eating any cooked food.

In situations where you're unable to eat raw food first, you can take a high-quality digestive enzyme supplement before eating cooked food. Two of the strongest enzymes on the market include DG-X by Theramedix and Quantum Digest by Premier Research Labs.

The Wind Up

Exercise your will power and your body's detox functions by "winding up" toward a raw food diet or cleansing phase. This can be a comfortable, rhythmic exercise that teaches you to "take a day off" from your dietary program whenever you get too stressed about it. This pattern is based on Dr. Haag's fat-loss program.

Day 1: Eat only living foods
Day 2: Eat anything you want, within reason
Days 3 & 4: Eat only living foods
Day 5: Eat anything you want, within reason
Days 6 thru 8: Eat only living foods
Day 9: Eat anything you want, within reason
Days 10 thru 13: Eat only living foods

Dr. Haag's program: On the days that you eat living foods, eat only one type of fruit and one type of fat (either seeds or avocado) on that day.

The Cleansing Cycle

The first time you do a cleanse, you will be "teaching" your body how to eliminate toxins it may have been holding onto your whole life. This is why most cleansing programs call for a longer cleanse the first time you do it. Even if you've done a cleanse before, you will see better results, and be more comfortable, if you ease into and out of the cleansing phase. Raw foods are perfect for this.

Days 1 thru 3: Eat only living foods

Days 4 thru 6 (or longer): Drink only fresh juices, or follow a cleansing program
Days 7 thru 9: Eat only living foods

During the cleansing days, you can focus on a colon cleanse, liver detox or a general cleansing protocol. See the Resources section for some cleansing program options.

Cold Turkey

Some people find that making slow changes is more difficult than jumping right in and following an extreme program. This could be based on personality factors or your propensity to binge eat certain foods. If this is the case for you, then remove everything you don't want to eat from your kitchen and fill your refrigerator with an abundance of fresh food. Go for it!

Baby Steps

Pick one of the practices listed below that feels doable for you and continue it for at least three weeks before focusing on another one. (As they say, twenty-one days make a habit!*) You can learn a lot about yourself and take baby steps toward better health by following any of these strategies, and you can keep a personal health journal to chart your goals and progress over time.

- Drink sour juice (gft, cran, sour apl) before eating Spritz salads and food with fresh lemon or lime
- Drink half your weight in ounces of water every day (i.e. 160 lb. = 80 oz.)
- Add fresh lemon juice to your water throughout day
- Eat raw food or take digestive enzymes before eating cooked food
- Eat fresh fruit first thing in the morning (30 min before anything else)
- Make large batches of smoothies and refrigerate in portions
- Eat your salads with raw dressings or top-quality oil and vinegar
- Eat nothing 3 hours before bedtime
- Eat an apple a day
- Eat your largest meal between 10:00 and 2:00 (midday or midnight)

- If you remove one type of food from your diet, be sure to add a new one as well
- Discover a new fruit every month
- Learn what types of food are locally grown and in season
- Eat ½ tsp of high-mineral sea salt every day
- Go on and off one type of food a few times so you can discern its effects (e.g. dairy products, wheat, corn, sugar, coffee, etc.)
- Eat in a quiet place with no distractions
- Spend more time chewing your food
- Eat meals with people you love
- Express gratitude and your intentions for better health before eating
- Spend time preparing a homemade meal at least once per week
- Drink one tablespoon of raw apple cider vinegar every morning to strengthen your digestion
- Add fresh leafy greens to your fruit smoothies
- Take a daily fiber supplement
- Get at least 15 minutes of sunshine every day, or watch the sunset
- Do a cardio exercise for 20-30 minutes three times per week
- Grow some of your own food in your yard or kitchen
- Grow and juice your own wheatgrass
- Germinate raw nuts and seeds (soak 12 hours in water) before eating or blending

FIND A BALANCE WITH RAW FOODS
From the *Free CD* by Jordan Maerin

What does it mean to be in "balance" with your health and diet? There are at least a few ways in which we use this word.

First, many people consider a diet to be "balanced" when it includes all the food groups, as laid out by the ADA in its famous food pyramid. The problem with this conception of balance is that it doesn't always work in the real world. As you probably know, there are many people who report feeling better, or losing excess weight, or healing from disease, simply by removing one or more of these food groups from their diets – for instance, grains, meat or dairy products. This is really a default definition of balance. It says, basically, that since we (the creators of the pyramid) don't really know what you should be eating, you should eat everything, just in case.

In a second sense, "balance" is used to describe a state of perfect health, with the contrast, disease, being a state of "imbalance." This definition, however, denies that disease serves any positive function – it's just simply wrong, something against which we actively fight or upon which we wage costly wars. What we seldom realize is that anything that hurts our disease also hurts us, for *our diseases are us.* Cancer is simply an overgrowth of our own cells, and viruses can just as easily be endogenous, created from within. This conception of balance could apply to temporary illnesses and uncomfortable detox phases, but what about chronic illnesses? Are chronically ill people simply "out of balance" their whole lives? This doesn't seem very helpful.

A third conception of "balance" is holistic – it acknowledges that at any given moment, our diet and health represent a perfect balance amidst all the dimensions and realities of our lives. That is, the diet I eat reflects both the *historical* and cultural context of my life, as well as the state of my body and mind at the *present* time, and my ability to manifest what I *imagine* to be my ultimate diet and state of health. As I experiment with diet, exercise and healing modalities, and gain knowledge, my balance shifts. It also shifts with changing life circumstances, such as my age, attitudes and beliefs, work and living circumstances, the amount of free time I have, and what else is going on in my life. Health issues also touch upon spirituality, the "bigger" questions, such as, "Is my life worth living?", "Do I belong here on this earth?" and "Is there a reason for this disease I've had for so long?"

> The body is the "perfect manifestation of complete being." - Susun Weed

Maintaining healthful practices each day requires hope, peacefulness, time, and self-love. How often do you give these gifts to yourself?

A fourth sense of "balance" is more practical, and includes elements of the first three. Many people considering a new diet ask, "What kind of diet will help me accomplish my goals, that I can actually maintain on an on-going basis and not feel that I am missing anything nutrition-wise?" This is a balance we feel with our daily practices, a *groove* we get into when we can forget we're on a diet – we are simply practicing new habits that work. This is a balance we maintain over time, usually with the understanding that it's a phase. How long it will last, we cannot know. When the balance is no longer felt, the seeking and shifting begin again. Then we either go deeper into some of our current practices, or we discover some new ones.

When we're seeking a new balance, it can help to have a vision, or at least a place to start. This is why raw food authors and teachers are so helpful. As you research answers to the question, "What does a balanced raw food diet look like?" you will notice a couple of things. First, there are many different answers to the question, and second, each chef or teacher will have different recommendations for exercise and healing modalities that they use in conjunction with diet to create a healthy balance. As a seeker, you must find or synthesize a balanced vision that matches your philosophies, beliefs, personality type, lifestyle, financial resources, etc. Then just start experimenting and find what works for you.

When I first discovered raw food, I decided I would eat 100% raw. I did this for three weeks and realized I was not able to find a balance because I had so much energy I couldn't sleep longer than about three hours a night. This was not a good balance for me mentally because I tend to be an anxious, hyper personality, and it was torture to be awake for longer than I was used to. I started eating a little cooked food with my dinner salads, eating all else raw throughout my day, and that's the balance I maintained for about four years.

During that time, my daily diet looked something like this:

MORNING: Citrus, or citrus juice, plus lots of water.

LUNCH: A rich smoothie with fresh coconut, hemp seeds, raw cacao, berries, fresh greens and green powder.

MID-AFTERNOON: Nuts and raisins, or energy bars, or flax crackers with avocado or sunflower pate.

DINNER: A large salad with a variety of garnishes, with A small amount of complex carbs, including baked potato, lentil or veggie soup, beans and brown rice, etc.

After that four-year phase, I started cooking for a living again. I also began focusing more on healing my emotional issues with food, since I was the child of an abusive home, where packaged TV dinners were served in a hostile, stressful environment. I felt that it was way too easy for me to go without eating, or to eat so little and be so skinny, and I wasn't sure this was a good thing in the context of my own story. Currently, my diet is in flux, partly due to a recent move and an erratic work schedule – eating anywhere from 40 to 80% raw on any given week - but I know that when the time comes, I'll settle into a new balance.

Whatever *your* story, it is an element of your uniqueness and your personal attitudes about food, its power and its possibilities, to this day. May you find a daily balance, in the fourth sense, while knowing that you always have a holistic balance, in the third sense.

> "Healing/health, the Wise Woman way is concerned with the story: the person's story, the family's tale, the community's fable, the planet's myth... By exposing the deeper roots of the tale, the wise woman grounds health... By creating anew the myth, the wise woman offers optimum nourishment."
> - Susun Weed, *Wise Woman Herbal: Healing Wise*

For further information or guidance, you can download or order Jordan's free CD, "How to Balance Your Diet," at www.eatfreshnow.com

TOP TEN TIPS FOR BUSY PEOPLE

1. Prepare larger batches of raw foods.

2. Forego machinery (easier clean up!).

3. Eat out - find the best salads, guacamole, fruit plates, etc., near you.

4. Frequent the other businesses near your favorite juice bars and health food stores.

5. Stash convenience foods (dried fruit, energy bars, apples) at work and in your car.

6. Locate raw foods on your daily route, from bananas at convenience stores to salad bars at commercial grocery stores.

7. Purchase ready-made foods, like flax crackers, raw cookies, granolas, etc.

8. Wash lettuce and veggies ahead of time and store them in your refrigerator until needed.

9. Multi-task while preparing recipes and marinating veggies.

10. Memorize your favorite recipes!

RESOURCES

·

INDEX

SUGGESTED READING

RAW INSPIRATION

Boutenko, Victoria. *12 Steps to Raw Foods: How to End Your Addiction to Cooked Food.*
Cobb, Brenda. *The Living Foods Lifestyle.*
Cousens, Gabriel, M.D. *Conscious Eating.*
Halfmoon, Hygeia, Ph.D. *Primal Mothering in a Modern World.*
Malkmus, George. *God's Way to Ultimate Health.*
Miller, Susie & Knowler, Karen. *Feel-good Food.*
Monarch, Matthew. *Raw Spirit.*
Nison, Paul. *Raw Knowledge II: Interviews with Health Achievers.*
Owen, Bob. *Roger's Recovery from AIDS.*
Szekely, Edmond Bordeaux, trans. *The Essene Gospel of Peace.*
Wolfe, David. *Eating for Beauty.*

RAW FOOD NUTRITION

American Natural Hygiene Society. *The Natural Hygiene Handbook.*
Boutenko, Victoria. *Green for Life.*
Cousens, Gabriel, M.D. *Depression Free for Life.*
Diamond, Harvey. *You Can Prevent Breast Cancer!*
Diamond, Harvey and Marilyn. *Fit for Life II: Living Health.*
Francis, Raymond, R.N.C., M.Sc.. *Never Be Sick Again: Health is a Choice, Learn How to Choose It*
Howell, Edward, Dr. *Enzyme Nutrition.*
Meyerowitz, Steve. *Sprouts: The Miracle Food.*
Meyerowitz, Steve. *Wheatgrass: Nature's Finest Medicine.*
Rose, Natalia. *The Raw Food Detox Diet.*
Shelton, Herbert M., Dr. *Natural Hygiene: The Pristine Way of Life.*
Walker, Norman, D.Sc., Ph.D. *Become Younger.*
Wigmore, Ann, Dr. *The Hippocrates Diet and Health Program.*

NATURAL FITNESS

Bazler, Thor. *Raw Power!: Building Strength and Muscle Naturally.*
Brazier, Brendan. *Thrive: A guide to optimal health and performance through plant-based whole foods.*
Graham, Dr. Douglas. *On Nutrition & Physical Performance.*
La Lanne, Jack. *Revitalize Your Life.*

RAW FOOD RECIPE BOOKS

Au, Bryan. *Raw in Ten Minutes.*
Baird, Lori, ed. *The Complete Book of Raw Foods.*
Calabro, Rose Lee. *Living in the Raw.*
Cornbleet, Jennifer. *Raw Food Made Easy.*
Cousens, Gabriel, M.D., and the Tree of Life Café Chefs.
　Rainbow Green Live Food Cuisine.
Juliano. *Raw: The Uncook Book.*
Malkmus, Rhonda J. *Recipes for Life from God's Garden.*
Markowitz, Elysa. *Warming Up to Living Foods.*
Mars, Brigitte. *Rawsome!*
Melngailis, Sarma, and Kenney, Matthew. *Raw Food Real
　World.*
Rhio. *Hooked on Raw.*
Romano, Rita. *Dining in the Raw.*
Shannon, Nomi. *The Raw Gourmet.*
Trotter, Charlie, and Klein, Roxanne. *Raw.*
Underkoffler, Renee Loux. *Living Cuisine: The Art and Spirit of
　Raw Foods.*

COLON HEALTH AND DETOXIFICATION

Anderson, Richard, N.D. *Cleanse and Purify Thyself.*
Krok, Morris. *Golden Path to Rejuvenation.*
Meyerowitz, Steve. *Juice Fasting and Detoxification.*
Morse, Robert, N.D. *The Detox Miracle Sourcebook.*
Walker, Norman, D.Sc., Ph.D. *Colon Health: The Key to a
　Vibrant Life.*

CLEANSING PROGRAMS

Arise & Shine, www.ariseandshine.com 1-800-688-2444
Dr. Schulze, www.herbdoc.com 1-800-HERB-DOC
EJUVA, www.ejuva.com (909) 337-5627
The Master Cleanser, www.mastercleanser.com

RAW LIFESTYLE MAGAZINES

Get Fresh! (UK), fresh-network.com
Health Science, (813) 855-6607 healthscience.org
Just Eat An Apple, fredericpatenaude.com
Purely Delicious Magazine, (919) 783-4050 purelydelicious.net
Vibrance ezine, (707) 829-0362 livingnutrition.com

VIDEOS & DVD'S

Butler, Aaron. *Simply Raw: Reversing Diabetes in 30 Days.*
Cohen, Alissa. *Living on Live Foods.*
Cousens, Gabriel, M.D. *Rainbow Green Live Food Cuisine.*
Day, Lorraine, M.D. *Cancer Doesn't Scare Me Anymore!*
Day, Lorraine, M.D. *You Can't Improve on God.*
Graff, Jackie and Gideon. *Nuts About Coconuts* and *Country Barbecue.*
Maerin, Jordan. *Raw Foods for Busy People DVD Premiere.*
Malkmus, George. *How to Eliminate Sickness.*

ONLINE RESOURCES

anhs.org: American Natural Hygiene Society website.
beyondhealth.com: Raymond Francis, healthy olive oil.
davidwolfe.com: Updated lists of raw restaurants.
essenespirit.com: Information about the Essene teachings.
excaliburdehydrator.com: Top of the line dehydrators.
goraw.com: Granola, flax crackers, energy bars.
living-foods.com: Internet educational community.
naturalhealthyconcepts.com: Premier Research supplements.
nesco.com: Simple dehydrators.
rawbakery.com: Gourmet desserts.
rawfamily.com: Instructional videos, books, food items.
rawfood.com: Sunfood Nutrition superstore.
rawfoodsnewsmagazine.com: Info and current events.
rawfoodlife.com: The science of raw foods.
rawpower.com: Protein powders and bodybuilding advice.
raw-pleasure.com: International raw directory.
sunorganic.com: Dried fruit, nuts, olives, flax products.
thegardendiet.com: Retreats and professional resources.
therawworld.com: Dr. Fred Bisci's online resource.
vita-mix.com: High horsepower blenders.

MAIL ORDER RESOURCES

Excalibur Dehydrators. 1-800-875-4254
Freeland Foods: Granola, snack bars. (619) 286-2446
Living Tree: Nut butters, etc. 1-800-260-5534
Mountain Home Basics: Appliances. 1-800-572-9549
Sun Organic Farm: Nuts, flax, olives. 1-888-269-9888
Sunfood Nutrition: All things raw. 1-888-RAW-FOOD

RAW FOOD RETREAT CENTERS

Creative Health Institute, Union City, Michigan
    creativehealthinstitute.us 1-866-426-1213
Hallelujah Acres (Christian), North Carolina and Ontario
    hacres.com 1-877-743-2589
Happy Oasis, Prescott, Arizona
    happyoasis.com (928) 708-0784
Hippocrates Institute, West Palm Beach, Florida
    hippocratesinst.org (561) 471-8876
Living Foods Institute, Atlanta, Georgia
    livingfoodsinstitute.com 1-800-844-9876
National Health Association, various locations
    www.anhs.org/community.htm (813) 855-6607
Nature's Raw Energy, Illinois
    www.naturesrawenergy.com (309) 755-0200
Optimum Health Institute, San Diego and Austin, Texas
    optimumhealth.org 1-800-993-4325
The Raw Retreat, Ojai, California
    www.therawretreat.com 1-877-236-6999
Sanoviv Medical Institute, Baja Coast of Mexico
    sanoviv.com 1-800-726-6848
Tanglewood Wellness Center, Frederick, Maryland
    tanglewoodwellnesscenter.com (301) 898-8901
Tree of Life Rejuvenation Center, Patagonia, Arizona
    www.treeoflife.nu (520) 394-2520

OTHER TITLES

Alimentos Crudos para La Gente Ocupada
Raw Foods for Busy People 2: Green Magic
Raw Foods for Busy People Premiere DVD
The Fresh Bartender: A Guide to Healthy Parties And Festive Juicing

Download
THE FREE CD:
How to Balance Your Diet
At www.eatfreshnow.com

Make it simple. Make it fresh. Make it Now!

Eatfreshnow.com is Jordan's *new* homepage, eaturing quick links, original articles and video demos, plus a **Free CD:** "How to Balance Your Diet."

Creative gifts and fan gear for gardeners, vegetarians and raw fooders.

ABOUT THE AUTHOR

Jordan Maerin holds a degree in Philosophy from Michigan State University and is the author of three recipe books and an instructional raw foods DVD. She is a raw food enthusiast, nature-lover and sungazer living in northern California.

Sometimes I think I understand everything, then I regain consciousness

Raw Foods for Busy People

Jordan Maerin 121

RECIPE INDEX

Jordan Maerin

A RAW FOOD BLESSING

I give thanks for the raw nutrients in this food, which I digest and absorb easily.

I give thanks for the living energy of this food, and in accepting it, I align myself with the generous energies of the Earth and Sun.

I give thanks for the nourishment of this food, which I accept openly, joyfully and righteously.

I give thanks for the divine illusion of this food, representing as it does the infinite cosmic energy of which I am a part.

I give thanks for this food as a tool of my intention to manifest my own strong, vibrant, comfortable body.

NOTES

NOTES

NOTES

NOTES

NOTES